MEMOIR

INFINITE
Miracles

KATIE SIMONS
MCCARTY

This book is a memoir. It reflects the author's present recollections of experiences over time. Some names and characteristics have been changed, some events have been compressed, and some dialogue has been recreated.

ISBN: 979-8-9895066-0-6 (paperback)

ISBN: 979-8-9895066-1-3 (eBook)

FRANKLIN SCHOOL
PRESS LLC

MASSACHUSETTS

First published in 2024 by Franklin School Press, LLC.

To Tim and PJ: I gave life to you, but your lives give me life. You are my miracles.

*For God did not give us a spirit of cowardice, but rather
a spirit of power and of love and of self-discipline.*

—2 Timothy 1:7

*I waited patiently for the Lord; he inclined to me and heard
my cry.*

—Psalm 40:1

in·fi·nite

adjective

1. limitless or endless in space, extent, or size;
   impossible to measure or calculate.

   "the infinite mercy of God"

2. another term for non-finite.

3. a space or quantity that is infinite.

(Definitions from *Oxford Languages*)

Dear Reader,

Infinite Miracles *is the three-part memoir of my journey as the mother of a medically fragile baby, Tim. As a "mature" mom who was going to be a first-time mom at age thirty-seven, I was ready, excited, and determined to perfectly balance my career and motherhood. So when I learned about my son's rare fetal diagnosis of an omphalocele, I was stunned. I entered the Stages of Grief Club and surrendered the expectations I had held for the perfect motherhood and perfect child.*

Little did I know that my personal transformation had just begun.

I had to adapt to a new medical environment and learn to speak a different language, one full of appointments, specialists, and medical moms like me. And then subtler shifts in my mindset began to happen. I began to interpret challenges as blessings and feel gratitude in the smallest moments. I also developed a powerful sense of perspective and new courage to endure. These small, gradual steps out of despair and the surrender of expectations were attributed to one thing: faith.

This is a story of faith and resilience. It is about my son who endured his first years in the hospital: fifty-four days in NICU and countless days on the pediatric floor and PICU. As I recount my story, God and Mary, the Mother of Jesus, are present through signs and prayer. In this story, I will use "God" as a simple way to express Him instead of different titles, like Our Father, Our Lord, the Son, Jesus, and the Holy Spirit. At times, it felt like God was with me as the Father and wise parent. Other times, I could feel God as the Holy Spirit through my feelings and coincidences. And other times it was the stories of Jesus (when God and humanity came together in Him) that inspired me with hope.

If you are a NICU parent reading this story, please know that I hope you find comfort, peace, and healing—for you and your baby—during your NICU journey. I also understand how hard it is to focus in the NICU, never mind read an entire book! So, at the very end of the book, I have organized all my reflections on NICU themes, such as expectations, suffering, anger, and joy, with page references so you can quickly flip to the section that most applies to your life right now.

The miracles I experienced during this time were the gift of life for our son and the faithful endurance to survive the journey. I learned that our everyday moments were infinite miracles. I gave life to Tim, but his life gave me life.

I hope you enjoy my story.

Your friend,
Katie

TABLE OF CONTENTS

PART I

THE PREGNANCY JOURNEY

CHAPTER 1
The Ultrasound

Life as I knew it was shattered at the twenty-week ultrasound. There was Katie before, and there is Katie now, and those two women could not feel more differently about life and trust and faith and sorrow and joy.

"It's not your fault," the sonogram technician said.

My husband, Chris, and I had breezed into what we thought would be a routine, twenty-week prenatal appointment to update us on a healthy pregnancy with a special highlight: the gender reveal. I was hoping for a boy.

After our two p.m. appointment, I was going to zip back into my new office in the Rocky Mountains foothills for a three-thirty meeting. But as I laid on the exam table, I quickly realized I wasn't going back to my office that day.

•

"It's not your fault," the sonogram technician said again. And she kept babbling to herself, "I haven't seen this in twenty years. Oh, my gosh. I'm so sorry. It's the universe. It's not your fault." Chris and I were terrified. As someone who is never at a loss for words, I was unable to speak, so I just grasped his hand.

Finally, I got my voice back. "What is going on? Please, what is going on?" My first thought was that the baby had died.

How can this be happening?

The sonogram technician crossed the room and grabbed a book. "I need my medical book. I need to call Dr. Long. Oh, wait—she's in L&D. I can't believe it. I haven't seen this in all my years as a sonogram technician. This practice has never seen this. I need my medical book."

Medical book? What was going on here? Is my baby alive? Does my baby have a deformity that is so rare that she, an experienced sonogram technician, needs to consult a book? Where is the doctor? Should the sonogram technician even be saying all of this? All these terrifying thoughts swirled in my brain.

Chris was squeezing my hand back, but I couldn't read his face. *Was he hearing the same news I was hearing? Why wasn't he reacting?* My anxiety and terror escalated with each second of this appointment. And the alarming—and now that I look back, shameful—thought that popped into my head: in that moment, I hoped that the baby was a girl, because I didn't want the son I dreamed of to be anything but a healthy, strapping boy.

The tech babbled on, "Oh, wait—I finally see genitals. It's a boy!" In her chaos and verbal stream of consciousness, I believe she meant to deliver this as good news. Instead, she created a storm of terror for me and Chris. I felt like I just received my second kick in the gut. *My precious boy. How can this be happening to the little boy I wanted so badly?* In the next breath, she stated, finally, what was happening: "It's an omphalocele."

"An um-what? What is that? *What is that?*" I begged, my voice regaining its strength. But Chris was on his phone. *How could he be on his phone right now?!* "How are you checking your email or texting right now? STOP!" I needed an emotional punching bag and he became the victim of my verbal blows.

Chris was typing furiously and didn't even look up when he said, "Katie, I am taking notes. I don't have a notebook. I need to take notes on my phone."

I apologized quickly and started to weep. First, this news, and now I was taking out my anger and sadness on him. I had been hit by a tidal wave of terrifying emotions and I was drowning.

I can't recall when the sonogram technician explained what this "um" condition was. It was such a long, foreign word— omphalocele (*um-fal-o-seal*)—that I was fixated simply on trying to say it and not trying to understand what it was. In my desperate attempt to calm myself down, I looked back at the sonogram screen and really focused. I could see the baby's head: a round head with a tiny, perfect nose. And there were his little hands with long fingers, just like E.T. And also like E.T., he had a strange tummy. But it wasn't the pot belly E.T. has. Rather, it looked like a bubble was growing out of his tummy. It looked like my baby was blowing a giant bubble from his tummy. Like he was a pregnant baby.

Finally, Dr. Long came in. I was relieved. Now, we would have a calm voice of experience in this chaotic situation. Or so I thought. Dr. Long was still dressed in scrubs as she had been paged and taken out of L&D. I wondered how she was taken out of L&D—maybe she was done delivering the baby and had a break or maybe someone else had taken over for her because talking to us was more important. Somehow, her here with us gave me great comfort and great alarm at the same time.

She breezed into the room, looked at the ultrasound on the big screen, and then, without pausing to read the room, she said unemotionally, "Oh yes. That's an omphalocele. I haven't seen one of these since medical school." Dr. Long was in her mid to late fifties. This was not good. A sense of dread overcame me, flashing from my gut out through my entire body. I felt as though my precious baby had just been given a death sentence. I thought that Dr. Long would be a calming force in the room; instead, she was a know-it-all who took our devastating news and presented it to us as though she were relaying a snippet of celebrity gossip. She turned to the sonogram technician and asked to see the medical book that was pulled out earlier.

I was in shock. Rageful, devastated. *Are these two for real? Are they looking at a medical encyclopedia to deliver this news to us? I thought this was a reputable practice; Dr. Long went to Duke Medical School. Is this a joke?*

Then Dr. Long came over to where I was lying down and gave me a big hug. "I'm so sorry," she said. "I'm just so sorry."

The room was spinning, and I couldn't catch my breath. At this point, the shock and anger turned to hysteria. "What is the 'um' thing? What is it? Will my baby live? Will my baby boy live?" I held onto the tiny hope that this was just a prenatal thing, no biggie. But I knew in my heart it wasn't.

I can't recall her response, but I know that I was not reassured. I didn't hear any words like, "This is a treatable condition." Nor did I hear, "We have amazing resources to deal with this sort of thing." All I heard was a doctor, in her scrubs, saying over and over how sorry she was and that she knew that I would be strong. She mentioned that we needed to see a high-risk doctor right away. She would leave the referral at the front desk for me and Chris to pick up. And then she left me, sobbing in Chris's arms.

But the appointment wasn't even over. The sonogram technician still had more images to take! And her ceaseless chatter didn't cease. "I need to get pictures of his head. Oh gosh . . ."

Between sobs, I choked out, "What? What now?"

"He has cysts on his brain. I'm so sorry . . . but, well, babies at this stage sometimes have cysts on their heads . . . but given the omphalocele . . . it's like fluid on his brain." She oscillated from it being a normal fetus thing to an abnormal symptom affiliated with omphaloceles. This went on for a solid minute—her wondering out loud if the cysts were normal or not. I didn't pass out. I stopped weeping. I was numb. This appointment, from start to finish, was the most devastating, shattering experience Chris and I had ever had, and she continued to kick us down with her unprofessional wonderings and trite platitudes.

"Do you want pictures of your little guy? I mean, many families after they hear news like this don't want the pictures."

It was the first time I let out my true voice.

"Yes, I want the damn pictures." Even in my shell-shocked state, I was a mom. And I wanted pictures of my baby.

She finished and left. I took five minutes to dress and compose myself before Chris and I left that devastating, horrible, very bad appointment.

Chris and I went home in shock and now had to tell the devastating news to our family. Our phones were blowing up during the entire appointment because we had a family bet about the gender of the baby and planned to text everyone immediately. When no one heard from us for hours after the appointment, they became worried.

Chris and I called my parents first, who live outside of Boston, and told them of this foreign condition that we couldn't even pronounce but that it started with "um" and we think we Googled it correctly and it looked like a pregnant baby. "Mom," I sobbed, "something is wrong with the baby's stomach, and it looks like he's blowing a bubble out of his tummy."

My mom didn't even react. Instead, she went into action mode. She put us on hold, grabbed her landline, and called her friend, Betsy, a former NICU nurse, to ask her what this "um" thing was. As this was happening, Chris called his parents, who live locally, and told them the news. We decided to drive over to their house so we were not alone during such a difficult time.

Meanwhile, Mom got back on the phone with us and patched my dad and Betsy into our phone call. Somehow, Betsy figured out that we meant omphalocele. Betsy brought the first feeling of calm in this emotional turbulence. "Katie and Chris," she said, "it's an omphalocele, and this is a fairly common thing. This is very treatable."

Through Betsy's description and our Googling—we finally figured out how to spell *omphalocele* well enough to type it into Google—I was learning, live, that an omphalocele is a condition in which a baby's organs grow outside of its body, covered only by a thin, transparent layer of tissue. And an omphalocele can often mean the baby has serious chromosomal or congenital abnormalities. It can also cause death. I had immediately catastrophized the situation.

My mind was spiraling out of control with questions for Betsy. "But what about the sonogram technician and the doctor who said the practice had never seen an omphalocele? Why did they refer to a medical encyclopedia in front of us? Google is showing me all the related syndromes affiliated with omphaloceles? Or what about Trisomy 18? Babies with Trisomy 18 have omphaloceles. I know he has Trisomy 18! Those babies don't live long—usually days—a year or two at the most."

Betsy stayed vigilant in her reassurance. "Katie, no. He has an omphalocele. That does not mean that he has other syndromes or conditions. You must take this one step at a time. Do you have another appointment?" We told her that we had an appointment the following day with the high-risk OBGYN practice. "Good," she said. "They deal with these conditions every day. You will see that this is highly treatable and that it is likely an isolated physical issue."

And I knew, deep down, that she was right. My mind recalled the images from the sonogram. I immediately retrieved my purse to get the sonogram picture that I had brought home from the appointment. As I looked at the photo, I found that my memory was correct: he had a perfect head, hands, and feet. It was just his tummy that was different.

Betsy had said to us what Dr. Long should have said. *Isolated. Treatable.*

We got off the phone, and for the first time since before the ultrasound, I felt a wave of peacefulness.

The calm and peace were short lived, of course, because the mind has a powerful way of wondering off into the what-ifs. I promptly drifted back into a sea of worry and dread after the momentary calm.

Looking back, I wish that I had taken time to pause and pray in my time of distress. But my relationship with God in those hours after the ultrasound was not as strong as it would become in the weeks and months to come. Like Jesus's disciples in the Sea of Galilee, I panicked when the furious storm of my life came upon my boat. But God was there—through Betsy and my family—telling me to pause on all the worry and be alert for information, and to have faith that it was, in fact, a treatable condition.

Chris hung up the phone on the last in the series of family calls, and we both slumped on the couch. Our selected boy name was Colin. Through my tears, I blurted out to Chris, "Chris, if this kid has stomach issues, we cannot name him Colin because I just keep thinking of the colon."

"Yes!" he exclaimed. "I actually thought the same thing! We can't name him Colin." And with that, we started Googling for the patron saint of medicine and surgery. We found Erasmus. We debated it for a minute or two.

"What are we thinking? We can't do that to the poor kid." Chris agreed.

And it was then that I Googled "patron saint of stomach issues" and found St. Timothy. Strange. At the time, the only Bible passage I knew by heart was from St. Paul's letter to St. Timothy: "For God did not give us a spirit of cowardice, but rather a spirit of power and of love and of self-discipline" (2 Timothy 1:7).

That felt perfect: Timothy.

The name change was our petition to God—Chris and I needed His divine help for healing our son. But the name change represented something else too: that feeling of certitude that we would have a healthy, strapping baby boy named Colin who would grow up to be an outgoing, happy, strong, smart, athletic, and kind man had been shattered. I had imagined Colin with a perfect fantasy life. I had projected my dreams and aspirations onto Colin. And now I realized that Colin didn't exist.

In fairness to myself, I think a lot of first-time parents do this. They project their unfulfilled dreams and ideal qualities onto their unborn child, sometimes even well into childhood, but over the course of time, they realize the child they have isn't the child they envisioned. It's true that many parents try to mold their kids into their mini-me, but eventually, even after the kids leave the nest, parents have to let them become their own selves with their own destinies. But for Chris and me, this process happened not over the course of months and years as most parents experience, but at warp speed. We had to completely alter our expectations—or rather, get rid of our expectations—about who our baby would be. And in that rapid process, we experienced simultaneous feelings of unconditional love and profound grief.

We were on the brink of new life and death, physically and metaphorically. I loved our baby, no matter what the condition, situation, or challenges we may face, but I was shattered with overwhelming grief that my baby was not the Colin I had envisioned. And with this grief came guilt because the former made me question my unconditional love. *How could I feel grief if I feel unconditional love?* It was confusing and messy.

And this is why we needed to petition to God and St. Timothy. There was no Colin; Tim was our boy.

Chris and I nodded to each other. Timothy.

CHAPTER 2
Why Me?

The ultrasound was the moment that my pregnancy went from one of innocence in which I used to think to myself, *What color will the nursery be and how will I lose the baby weight after baby is born?* to now a much more serious and alarming experience: *How do I get up to speed with all this medical stuff? Will the baby be able to come home with us after he's born? Will I have to exit my career to take care of such a fragile, medically complicated baby?* And for all this—our loss of an innocent, easy pregnancy, and a newfound complicated medical journey for our family—I was angry at God. *How could you do this to me?*

I was thirty-seven years old, and I was having my first baby. Like the biblical matriarchs and heroines who had babies in their advanced ages, like Sarah and Elizabeth, it felt like a small miracle that I was even pregnant because, while we may not want to admit it, it can be harder to get pregnant as we get older. To add to the pain, I felt that I had paid my dues: I had attended countless baby showers for my friends, wondering when my turn would come. I covered for everyone else's maternity leaves. I finally got married later in life, and we were starting the family of which I had always dreamed. *And this? This is how it is happening for me?*

I can't remember if I took the time to say these things directly to God, but it's how I felt in those early days. I felt entitled to have a happy, easy pregnancy because it was *my turn*. As I would learn through the pregnancy, the birth, and the subsequent trials, that is not how life or parenthood works. It is our trials that define us, make us stronger, and lead us to be better parents than we ever thought we could be.

But at the time, I hadn't learned those lessons. At the time, I unleashed my anger on God. *Why me? Why us? Why our little boy?* I felt entitled to an easy pregnancy, but at the same time, I was begging God to know the reasons why I'd been dealt such a difficult hand. Like Job, I begged God to tell me what I did wrong to deserve this pain. I know now, many years later, that searching for answers for suffering is a futile exercise because there is no way to know God's ways and His plans for us. But at that time, that's what I felt: confusion

Entitled, yet begging. Mistreated, yet wanting understanding. *What have I done wrong to deserve all this? How can this be happening to me?*

The anger clouded most positive feelings, except one glimmer of hope: the one good thing that stuck in my mind from the ultrasound—and was verified by that precious photograph I'm so glad I took home—was that each one of his fingers and toes looked perfect. Once the technician and doctor pointed out the omphalocele on the big screen where we were viewing the sonogram, I saw *it*, of course: the omphalocele that looked like a giant bubble of Big League Chew blowing out of his tummy. But then my gaze shifted to his perfectly round head and fully formed fingers and toes. They weren't webbed or malformed. I had no medical training, nor had I had a baby before, but something in my gut and my heart said, *He's okay. It's just a bubble tummy, and they will fix it. He doesn't have anything else because his head and fingers and toes perfect.* That was my gut instinct, felt in a split-second moment, but then I doubted it for the rest of the appointment. The reaction of the technician and doctor overwhelm my and I was overcome by grief, anxiety, and terror.

Hours and days later, I remembered. I remembered the fingers and toes. And I had the good sense to take that photograph home. My glimmer of hope.

The night before the appointment with the high-risk practice was one of only two nights (the second night was right before our baby boy was born) during my pregnancy that Chris and I didn't sleep. Couldn't sleep. Our minds were spinning with the news. We could feel the other tossing around. Throughout the night, we would turn to each other and say, "Are you having trouble sleeping?" I can't remember what we talked about, but it was the peak of our vulnerability with one another—we talked, we cried, and finally in the middle of the night, we prayed.

Chris was the one who suggested that we pray. He had become Catholic the year before through RCIA (Rite of Christian Initiation of Adults) and, in many ways, he was more pious than me, the "cradle Catholic" who had attended the College of the Holy Cross and been raised by a strong Irish-Catholic mom and "Captain Catholic," my dad who made us to go to Mass even on vacation. I agreed with Chris: we should pray. I was secretly angry with God, but I also knew that it was okay to reveal my true feelings to Him. Over the course of the pregnancy, God would soften my heart, and my anger would dissipate. But I wasn't there yet.

I agreed to pray anyway. We sat in the darkness, reciting the Lord's Prayer, hoping to find respite from the thrashing anxiety. We prayed the Lord's Prayer together dozens and dozens of times until we gently fell asleep around dawn.

A few hours later, our alarm woke us up. Because of our anxiety about the appointment at the high-risk practice, my mother-in-law, Susan, was going to drive us and be a third set of ears during the appointment. I was getting dressed, and I asked Chris to zip up my dress. "Katie, um, I don't know how to say this, but your dress won't zip up." I had popped! I finally had my pregnancy pop! We both laughed, relieved to have such a normal pregnancy milestone in the middle of our turmoil.

I found a looser dress, and Susan pulled up in front of our apartment building. It was a short drive to the high-risk practice, which was very different from my other OBGYN office—more staid and quieter, whereas the other office was colorful, fashionable, and bustling with a lot of conversation. But it didn't bother me; the quietude of this new office comforted me.

This appointment would be an hour-long anatomy scan. We were greeted by a new sonogram technician, Kristin. Immediately, I became tense as a flood of bad memories from our horrible sonogram the day before rushed in. But we could not have asked for a more opposite person; the day prior, our sonogram technician chatted endlessly, thinking out loud when she should have been silent and focused. Kristin was instead quiet, serious, and aware of the trauma we had experienced. She introduced herself, told us about her credentials and experience, and then explained that she would not talk during the anatomy scan because she had to navigate the tiny baby parts—from head to toe—with careful attention. "So, when I am quiet, it doesn't mean anything is bad," she summarized.

Sure enough, Kristin carefully looked at our little boy from the tips of his toes, up to his organs growing on the outside of his body, to his heart—all four quadrants in excruciating detail—to the top of his beautiful head. Occasionally, she would look up and reassure us that all was going well and not to be worried. Then Dr. Hatch, a tall, older man, walked in the room to introduce himself. He excused himself to debrief with Kristin and then we all regrouped to take another look with the doctor as he told us the results. This was everything that our other ultrasound should have been—calm, quiet, and professional.

Dr. Hatch finally began, "Yes, it is an omphalocele. And we see omphaloceles all the time. You are in the right place. We will be taking care of you from now on. Right now, we can see that your baby's liver and intestines are growing outside of his body. The good news is that we are not seeing any other issues, so there is a strong possibility that this is an isolated, physical condition. It is very treatable, and many omphalocele babies grow up to have healthy, normal lives. But I want to make *sure* that it's just an isolated condition, so I suggest we do an amnio so we can be absolutely sure."

Prior to the appointment, I wasn't aware that it was even a possibility to have an amniocentesis (often referred to as an *amnio*) during this appointment, especially this late—twenty weeks—in the pregnancy. And I am very glad I didn't know, because if I had known about it the evening prior, I wouldn't have even slept those few precious hours.

An amnio is an invasive procedure in which the doctor takes a long needle and inserts it in the pregnant belly to extract the amniotic fluid to be tested to find out if there are certain birth defects. I was terrified. I didn't know a lot about amnios, but I knew a really long needle had to go into my belly and it was late in the pregnancy to be doing such an invasive procedure. The office calculated the pregnancy math and it was, indeed, the *last day* we could safely do an amnio. *What if the needle pierces my baby or causes so much trauma that I miscarry? And what if I find out bad news?* It's a gut-wrenching decision that affects the entire pregnancy.

Dr. Hatch addressed my first concern about potential miscarriage. "There is always risk, but it is a very small percentage."

And then the big issue: abortion. For me, the outcome of the amnio wasn't going to affect the pregnancy in terms of a decision to abort the baby if we found out devastating news, like the baby has severe chromosomal abnormalities or terminal prognosis. "But Dr. Hatch, I don't see the point of the amnio because no matter what the results are, I will not do an abortion. It is against my conscience and my faith."

"I'm also a Christian," he reassured me. "And I'm not suggesting abortion. Just by spending the appointment with you two for the past hour or so, I have the feeling that you won't like all the wondering about the outcomes for your baby for the duration of your pregnancy if you don't do the amnio. Let's be sure. Let's do the amnio."

I had to make a decision on the spot. I, like the office, knew the math on the pregnancy. There was no wiggle room for an amnio after twenty weeks. In other words, I couldn't say to Dr. Hatch, "Thank you for your opinion, but I would like to think about it for a few days and if we decide to do it, I will make an appointment for next week." No, I had to decide right then and there. I was scared and confused. "I'm still worried," I told him.

"I'm not. I do these every day," he replied.

Because I could feel that he wouldn't suggest (at best) or advocate (at worst) for an abortion based on the results, I trusted his words and felt his faith. I decided to do it.

I requested that the lights stay off during the amnio because I was terrified of the long needle. Dr. Hatch respected that request and performed the amnio in the dark. Now that I look back on it, he really must have done amnios every day because God only knows how he was able to see anything in that dark room: a leap of faith for all of us.

Chris and I left the appointment feeling more centered and calm because we had the right doctors in place. But there was still so much fear and uncertainty, especially since we would have to wait three weeks for the results. Now we were part of a new club: the high-risk pregnancies. And that term— *high risk*—sounded so scary. There were so many unknowns for us. *Is this an isolated, physical issue that can be treated and healed so our son can live a healthy, normal life? Or will we have a very serious situation with a chromosomal disorder and a severely handicapped child with physical limitations and cognitive difficulties? Or are we to face the unthinkable—a child born with a terminal prognosis?*

For three anxious weeks, Chris and I waited to find out the results of the amnio. It wasn't going to be easy to be patient and stay strong. It felt like the rest of the lives of all three of us were going to be determined by a single phone call.

CHAPTER 3
Speaking Words of Wisdom

Before I found myself in the West, I lived in New York City for ten years. I didn't dream of NYC as a little girl or make it a life goal to live there as many do; it just happened. I grew up outside of Boston, went to college in Massachusetts, and moved to Boston post-college. Then I felt I needed a change, and New York had the right opportunity—a teaching fellowship—and the bigger city that I craved.

Many poets and writers can describe all the wonders, beauty, chaos, insanity, heartbreak, and drive of New York City much better than I can, so I will just say that New York intoxicated me. I loved the buzz, the anonymity, the endless fun, and the grit. Because the city never stops, I never stopped. And that's probably why I didn't realize, even after several years, that I wasn't happy there anymore. Over time,

I was drinking, partying, dating the wrong men, and slowly falling into the debauchery of New York. It's hard to believe, if you've never lived in New York, that you can go out at midnight, party until three a.m., stumble home, and wake up whenever you feel like weekend after weekend and not think something is off. Sometimes, these nights happen during the week too; the night life is so intoxicating that it's hard to be disciplined to go home after work.

At the same time, I always envisioned myself as a career woman first who would marry at age thirty. We would have a few kids. I would be a working mom who somehow kept a gorgeous home, a kick-ass career, a happy husband, and cute, quirky kids. That was my vision. My generation was the first to have this carrot dangled in front of us—the carrot that you are a superwoman who can do it all and do it very well. I wanted this imaginary life so badly.

That's when God called me. Well, he hit me over the head with a holy wooden two-by-four and shouted, "Enough. Enough of New York. Enough of imagining a fantasy life." And I finally listened. And over time, after living there for ten years, and with the help of Spiritual Direction (a Jesuit practice), mentors, and retreats, I finally left NYC for a life out West. I was longing for some peace and quiet.

When I moved out West, things fell into place almost immediately. At first, I was in a state of euphoria that I had never experienced in my life. And I was aware of it. I remember seeing the magnificent mountains ahead of me as I drove one day, and I pulled over to take them in and thought, *I want this happiness to last forever,* because I knew it wouldn't. Simultaneously, I had a feeling of profound sadness because I thought, *Why is my life coming together now, so far from all my family and friends? Should I have done this sooner?* I was thirty-five, and I felt that things were finally falling into place. The pressure of life timelines had always stressed me, even at a very young age, and thirty-five felt too old to feel so unsettled.

I met Chris almost immediately through a mutual friend, Cynthia. We fell for each other instantly. We had a whirlwind romance, got married, and I got pregnant right away. We were entering into a life that I had always wanted, that I had always dreamed about. And I was pregnant with a baby we both desperately wanted.

But now there was a catch, a big one: our precious baby had a rare birth defect. And we had to wait three long weeks for test results that would impact the course of all our lives. This sudden departure from what I envisioned shocked me to the core and can only be called trauma. Anyone who has experience with trauma knows that life doesn't stop when one has a traumatic experience, and that may be one of the hardest parts—how quickly the rest of the world moves on.

At the time, I was someone who had few boundaries with my colleagues, family, or friends and tended to overshare, so I found it difficult to decide how much or how little to tell people. These days I am much better at taking my worries, my suffering, my trials to God first. In my meditation I try to regularly "give it to God." I see myself handing over pieces of paper with each worry written on it, or if it's a big worry, I envision it as a giant boulder I'm heaving over to God. "Here, take it, please!" But back then, I had a hard time discerning what to share with others, often thinking they could solve my problems or ease my worries. It was no secret around the office that I was pregnant. But this was a new, complicated detail, and there was no way I could hide it. *So how would I tell people?*

I told the news to my boss, Mike, right away. In fact, he was the first person I contacted once we heard the news because I had to tell him that I couldn't make my three-thirty meeting back at the office. Mike was a great manager and friend; I felt little apprehension being transparent in my emotions when telling him that we had a serious issue with our little guy. He immediately said, "Take all the time you need." No questions asked.

But after the amnio the next day, I knew it was time to go back to work. If I stayed home, I would be all alone, and my thoughts would go rogue to an unhealthy place. So, back to work I went. I am a very cheery, talkative person, always flittering about the office. I knew that I wouldn't be my usual self at work, so I decided to get ahead of it. Slowly, I shared the news about the omphalocele with my colleagues.

But it was not an easy process. Many who are going through a traumatic experience face the evolving issue of what to tell people, what not to tell people, and how to communicate (or not communicate) on social media. For many of us, it feels like every word said or written has to be planned. I opted to create some talking points for friends, work colleagues, and even strangers about what I was going through. After all, I was visibly pregnant. I wanted to have answers prepared when people, especially those close to me, asked questions.

On top of dealing with grief and the challenge of communicating the trauma, I also had to prepare myself to absorb the responses of the recipients. I was completely blindsided by how often people with good intentions said something completely unhelpful and off-putting. I couldn't find a way to properly describe these people until one night when I was watching the show *Nashville*. The character, Scarlett, was going through the trauma of caring for her sick mother who had cancer. During one of the conversations with a doctor (who would become her boyfriend, naturally), he observed that she felt fatigue and stress because of all the "optimism bullies" around her—the people who don't listen and tell you that everything is going to be okay when it's not okay. Optimism bullies also fixate on silver linings when there aren't any.

Oh, my goodness! That was it! It was early on, but I knew I was about to have optimism bullies in my life too. Sure enough, they arrived in force:

"Katie, you look amazing. You must be so excited about having your little dude."

"I am. I am excited. But as you know, he has a pretty serious birth defect. I just take it one day at a time."

"Oh, Katie. Stop. He will be fine! You need to stop worrying so much. I bet he will be in and out the hospital in no time. When is your shower? And what is your plan for the nursery? What colors are you doing? And oh—the UppaBaby is the best stroller ever. You need to get it. And Katie, just think—when he's in the hospital, the stress of it will help you lose the baby weight! Katie, really. Stop worrying and start thinking about the positive stuff. Everything is going to be fine. The little dude will be a champ!"

Here is what I wished I had said: "I'm not sure you understand—my baby's organs are *outside of his body*. This is really serious stuff. This isn't a matter of a few days in NICU. This is a matter of months. This is not a baby with a little jaundice who needs some time under the lamp. This is a baby who will have major, major surgery within hours of his first breath. And I don't care about a dumb nursery! An UppaBaby stroller? They cost a fortune. Do you understand the type of medical bills we are going to have? And the 'silver lining' in all this is that I will lose weight faster? Are you kidding me?"

But I never said any of that. Instead, I just nodded and agreed with the optimism bully when they told me not to worry so much. "Yes, you are right. He's a fighter, all right," and I would sigh.

Then, there were people who tried to empathize, but they didn't quite understand that our situations were not the same. I called these people "over-empathizers." An over-empathizer is similar to an optimism bully, but they wanted to either one-up the story or compare the experience to the experience of someone they knew. Usually, the comparison was way off, and it made for an awkward conversation. Here is how to tweak the conversation above for an over-empathizer: take out the stuff about the material goods and instead add this sentence: "I totally know what you are going through. My sister's baby had a really bad cold when she was six months old, and she is doing great now!"

I honestly couldn't even respond to the over-empathizers except to choke the words, "Oh, great. I'm glad your niece is okay."

Last, there were the platitude people. They relied on platitudes and clichés to navigate a conversation. Here were the top platitudes that I heard during my journey:

"It is meant to be."

"It could be worse."

"It's God's plan."

"God only gives you what you can handle."

"God only gives hardships to the strongest people."

I didn't want to be strong. I wanted to have an innocent, exciting pregnancy where I registered for cool stuff and my biggest worry was when we would have the "sip and see." *Was this really God's plan? Did He look through the whole list of pregnant women and their husbands and say, "Ah, look! There's Katie and Chris. They are pretty tough, and they can handle a lot of crap. And it might be a good lesson in empathy and compassion for them. So, let's give them a baby with a serious birth defect because they can handle it, whereas Kara and Josh would never be able to handle having a child with a birth defect."*

In my heart, I knew people weren't saying these dismissive, clichéd things to be mean. In fact, I believe intentions were good. People don't know what to say when someone is navigating an unbelievable and traumatic experience, so I tried not to be so hard on people. After all, the common element to all these types is a desire for a more comfortable conversation. But it's important to realize this: suffering happens to all of us at some point in our lives, and we need to sit in that uncomfortable space because suffering isn't comfortable.

Early in the pregnancy, a wise friend said to me, "I will sit and listen to you. And I may be uncomfortable because I don't have the right thing to say, but I will be there for you in that moment. I need to be okay with being uncomfortable because that's how friends help friends through grief." She was right: we must allow grief the space to happen instead of giving a pep talk, or comparing to one's own experience, or offering a trite platitude to make everything better because it *doesn't* make it better. It makes it worse.

The keys to helping someone navigate a difficult situation are, in my experience, listening and gift-giving. Listening is the best, and gift-giving is the next best. If someone is going through a difficult time, give them a small gift. And it can be anything: a small box of chocolate, a five-dollar gift card for coffee, or even a text that says simply: *I'm thinking about you.* Those little acts of kindness touch the heart of the suffering person. And don't ask what to bring over, just bring it over because the person in pain doesn't even know what they want. So, if someone is going through a hard time, listen to them, and the next day, don't ask, just bring over a lasagna.

And I need to be honest—before all of this happened to me, I was an optimism bully, over-empathizer, and platitude person all in one. I bet I have said to someone, all in one conversation, "Everything will be okay. I know how you feel; my friend went through it too, and she came out stronger than before! After all, God only gives you what you can handle." I bet I said all that crap! And that's why I try not to be so hard on people. Also, I am still working on my listening skills. I have been in situations in which friends, indeed, have it "worse" than me. And I work hard to listen to their experience instead of offering a comparison to my journey (especially if it's similar) or offering trite platitudes, because when I do that, I minimize their experience and their feelings.

I had to temporarily cut some people out of my life because this sort of dialogue was not emotionally healthy for me. And I didn't want to give pious lectures all the time, telling friends or family to quit giving me a pep talk or listening to their sister's boyfriend's uncle's traumatic baby story. I'm happy to say that I am still friends with the optimism bullies, over-empathizers, and platitude people, but I just needed a break from them. For a while.

So, navigating my communication plan at work was especially challenging because I couldn't really take a break from coworkers.

My role, at the time, was to sell Educational Professional Services remotely from the western regional office to school districts in the Northeast. (Yes, I lived out West to work back East.) So, the colleagues with whom I worked the most were "phone colleagues." It was easier to fake a cheery voice on the phone, so I was judicious as to which "phone colleagues" I told. But I knew I had to tell Lisa.

Lisa was my field representative in the Philadelphia Metro area. She went to Holy Cross like me, albeit at different times. We shared a special bond through our common experiences: our upbringing, our alma mater, our faith, and our work ethic. I never told her, but I thought of her like the big sister I never had. But as I was soon to discover, Lisa would become much more than a mentor and work colleague. She set the foundation for how I was to handle this difficult news of a serious birth defect and difficult pregnancy. Looking back, I feel so grateful to God that He put Lisa in my life at that time.

I called Lisa and told her my news. I broke down into tears as I explained the condition and potential complications. She calmly listened and let me get it all out. It was then that she shared that her ten-year-old son, Brian, had an ultra-rare kidney disease. She was able to share this news with me without trying to one-up me or to over-empathize. Rather, it felt like she was gently telling me that life isn't always fair or perfect and that there is, indeed, suffering during our time on earth and it's particularly hard when it's our children who have to suffer. I felt a huge mix of emotions: sadness and sympathy for Lisa and her family, relief that I wasn't the only one with a sick kid, anger that such suffering happens to good people, and a sense of peace because her faith is iron strong and I felt that she could somehow transfer it to me.

"Lisa, how do you sleep at night when you have so much t worry about?" I asked.

"I do the Hail Mary over and over and over until I asleep. Do your Rosary, say your Hail Marys. Pray to every night, Katie. This is bigger than you or me. Tu over to Mother Mary and to God." This prayer plan, th our common bond and fellowship, proved to be one of the greatest gifts, not just for my pregnancy, but for my life. And it actually let me sleep at night.

It was a strange coincidence because my own mother had recently given me the Mary Medallion worn by my great-grandmother. I started to wear the necklace, would go on to wear it my entire pregnancy, and began doing as Lisa said: praying to Mary.

As I prayed, I developed my relationship with Mary. I had entered motherhood and now was asking Mary to mother me through it. But it wasn't so easy for me.

Because I had been single well into my thirties, I turned my back on "boring Mother Mary," who I associated with every calm, domestic moment that my life lacked (though I wanted it so badly). At the peak of my party-girl NYC days, I saw Mary as a stay-at-home mom who had little ambition and aspirations for herself, sacrificing everything for everyone else, and well, just not being any fun. I doubled down on my career and mocked those who stayed home, lived for baby showers, or talked about how their kid was student of the month. I look back at myself now and see that I was sad, jealous, and insecure that those milestones weren't happening for me. And my envy may have been masking a much larger issue—my worthiness—something I would have to confront head-on once my baby was born.

So, it was hard to turn to Mother Mary now; I hadn't exactly been nice or pleasant to her. But now I needed her, so I followed Lisa's advice and prayed to Mary every night during pregnancy. I still endured distress, but I knew that it was beyond my control and that my job was to stay strong and positive for my boy and to ask Mary for peace and strength to be a good mom and for Mary to mother me during this storm of my life and the life inside of me. Mary would do the rest.

"Hail Mary, full of grace.

the Lord is with thee.

Blessed art thou amongst women

and blessed is the fruit of thy womb, Jesus.

Holy Mary, Mother of God,

pray for us sinners,

now and at the hour of death.

Amen."

And she was there for me. I was humbled to my very core that she took me back and enveloped me into her arms like I was a small child. I needed help. I needed compassion. I needed Mary. It's important for me to share my relationship with Mary because she was—and still is—there for me throughout this whole pregnancy journey and as I became a new mom.

At night, I turned to Mother Mary as my emotional support through prayer. During the day, I looked to Lisa as my beacon of light and hope. But not in the traditional sense. We didn't talk about our worries and sorrow and grief. Instead, we worked! We were working on a sizable sales deal together and had to focus on all the details so we would close it. I believe God put us together on this deal to get our minds off our suffering and to leave our trials to Him. Our job was to stay the course, be focused, positive, and busy.

My Nana (named Mary) always said, "When you are depressed or sad, wash the kitchen floor." In other words, stay busy so your mind doesn't wander. I don't want to minimize depression in any way because I know it is a serious illness. But for me—who doesn't suffer from depression—it was better to keep busy and active for the majority of the day than to obsess about negative outcomes and allow the pain and hurt to consume me. Without speaking about it openly, I sensed that Lisa had the same mindset.

A few weeks after the omphalocele diagnosis, I was scheduled to fly to Philadelphia. Chris and I still hadn't heard back about the results of our amnio, and there was a possibility that the results would come back when I was in Philly. Mike, my manager, knew that I was going through a lot and left it up to me about the trip. "Katie, you don't have to go on this trip. Lisa can cover the meeting and won't think twice about it." But Chris and I discussed it and decided that it was best that I go. The first reason was that I would be with Lisa, and she would be the best emotional support I could possibly have. The second reason was that Chris knew this deal kept my mind sharp and away from negative thoughts. Also, it was an opportunity to visit Children's Hospital of Philadelphia (CHOP), the world leader in dealing with omphaloceles. I wasn't sure if I would have time to visit CHOP, but the mere thought of the opportunity to do so made it a no-brainer. I went on the trip.

And there was one other special part of the itinerary: a visit with my great-aunt, my grandfather's sister, Sister Genevieve. At the time, Sister Gen was ninety-five years old, and she would ultimately live to one hundred and two. Sister Gen had over ninety nieces and nephews (one of whom was my dad) and about fifty great-nieces and -nephews. And every year she wrote each one of us a birthday card in perfect cursive that only nuns can achieve. I don't know what was more impressive—her prolific writing or her impeccable script! Sister Gen had a magical quality that made you feel special, and her joyful countenance was contagious.

I was hoping that I could see Sister Gen because it had been at least five years since my last visit with her; and Lisa, who was educated by the same order of nuns of which Sister Gen was a part, insisted I see her. Now that I reflect, I see that God intentionally made this visit with Sister Gen happen because why her of all people to be the one to visit or see? I hadn't seen my immediate family in months, nor did I see close friends from back East on this trip. It was Sister Gen that God wanted me to see.

I entered the beautiful convent outside of Philadelphia, and the nuns cheerfully welcomed me in, doting on me. They brought me to Sister Gen's room, and she embraced me and loudly summarized (because her hearing was poor) in front of all the sisters, "This is Katie. My brother Jake's granddaughter. She grew up in Massachusetts, but she lives out West now. And now, she's going to have a baby boy! Her mom and dad told me all about it!"

"But Sister Gen . . . ," I replied, unsure. I wanted to tell her that the baby had a rare birth defect and we were waiting to find out if he would have any genetic issues that would impact his life, or if the condition was life-threatening.

"Are you talking? Speak louder, Katie. Did the rest of you hear? She's going to have a baby boy! Katie, come on. Let me introduce you to Sister Mary Frances. MARY!"

Sister Gen didn't let me finish what I wanted to explain. She spent the next hour showing me off to the sisters, who were so excited about my precious baby boy.

Sometimes I wonder if Sister Gen *did* hear me but interrupted me because she didn't want me to focus on the sadness, anger, and despair I felt. And I know that she likely knew about the omphalocele from my parents but pretended not to know so I could have respite from the constant anxiety of waiting for the results of the amnio. The visit with Sister Gen and her fellow sisters was the first time in a long time that I felt like a happy, pregnant woman. Her exuberance—

even at the age of ninety-five—allowed me to forget about the hardship and feel the joyful anticipation of pregnancy. For a few precious hours, the omphalocele was forgotten. And I needed that.

I know now that Sister Gen and her fellow sisters were my prayer warriors, working overtime to ask God for a safe delivery and healing for me and my newborn son. They even added Tim to the IHM Spiritual Treasury, which meant the nuns prayed for him during every Mass and communal prayer for a year. I mention this because, many years later, I connected my NICU story with my Grandma Simons's story. In 1961, she delivered my Uncle Larry three months prematurely. I asked my Auntie Kathy, Larry's wife, how he survived. She responded, "Who knows. They didn't have NICU back then. I really think Sister Gen and the nuns praying around the clock had a large part in keeping him alive." I think the petition of Sister Gen and her fellowship may have had a hand in Tim's miraculous story too.

I wish I had asked for more help and more prayers during this challenging time, but I feel grateful that others added me to their prayer lists even though I didn't ask them to. Instead, I tended to isolate myself and focus on my own prayers to God. But it is true that community can help the road feel a little less uphill. And communal prayer works! After I spent time with her, I felt like everything would be okay—a peace I hadn't felt since before the omphalocele diagnosis.

Back in work mode, Lisa and I prepared vigorously for the meeting. We met for dinner, and it was a huge comfort to see her in person. Here she was, dealing with her own son's devastating diagnosis, and she was beautiful, put together, and calm. I never told her directly, but she was my inspiration for everything. I wanted to be Lisa. And I was; when my son was in NICU, I got dressed and had makeup on each day so I could keep it together.

I can't remember exactly when I got the call—before or after our successful business meeting—but I got the call about the amnio results when I was driving past the King of Prussia Mall. I heard the phone ring. And I saw that it was a western area code: it was the high-risk pregnancy doctor's office. I can't believe I did this, but I picked up the phone while I was driving. The news was good: The omphalocele had no other related syndromes and no genetic issues!

I quickly pulled over to digest the news. I was overcome with relief, joy, and gratitude that the amnio results came back with the best possible outcome given the situation: an isolated, physical issue that could be repaired and allow our son to live a healthy, normal life. In my gut, I knew that would be the diagnosis because, after all, I had that strong feeling about his perfectly round head and fully formed fingers and toes. But I felt relieved to have the official results instead of relying on my intuition or false hope throughout the pregnancy. *My baby boy is okay! We are going to be okay!*

Of course, I knew that we had a long journey ahead of us, and fortunately, I didn't know how even an isolated omphalocele can have difficult consequences. But in that moment, I felt only peace and joy—from the excellent news and from the visit with the nuns. I called Chris right away. "Chris, there aren't any other issues. He's going to be okay." I could feel his relief over the phone, fifteen hundred miles away. And then, I called Lisa and told her the news as well. She was earnestly happy for us and this good news.

We had overcome one important hurdle. Now it was time to meet our son's new medical team and prepare for what would inevitably follow his birth: a NICU stay. For how long, we didn't know.

CHAPTER 4

*In Dr. Shapiro,
Not Dr. Google, We Trust*

I never had the chance to visit CHOP; the trip to Philadelphia was short, and I didn't want to take advantage of my company's travel policy to do personal business. But over the next month, Chris and I busily gathered information and followed up with resources to find the best care route for our baby boy. We decided that we would do anything to improve the outcomes for our son, even if it meant moving. And the two places that were on the radar were Philadelphia, for CHOP, and Boston, for Boston Children's Hospital, ranked the number-one children's hospital in the country.

Boston was the obvious choice. My parents live outside of the city. My company was based in Boston. And though it would be harder for Chris with his role in the federal government, we were hopeful he could transfer to the Tip O'Neill

Building in downtown Boston if we really needed to. Chris and I had a strong support system in Boston because we both went to college in Massachusetts. Chris's family lived locally, but I was new to the area and hadn't put down many roots. So it wouldn't be too hard to leave, even though we were both happy there.

But since we couldn't move at that moment, we had to keep up my current prenatal care team for the time being. The high-risk practice set us up with a tour of their partner hospital to meet with the doctors and nurses there, though I was so set on moving back to Boston that the meeting didn't really carry much importance to me. "Let's do this tour as a courtesy to our current care team because they have been so amazing the past couple weeks," I said to Chris. "But remember—they want our business, and we need to be picky buyers." I intentionally left out: *We will be moving to Boston anyway, so who cares about this hospital.*

I realize now that I had a rather detached and businesslike approach to our situation. Yes, there were moments of intense faith and people who came into our lives that reflected the wisdom and peace of God and Mary. But there was also the rational part of me that kept detached and focused on work because the weight of our situation was so heavy.

On a sunny morning in late October, we arrived at Western Regional Pediatric Hospital (WRPH) for early meetings and a whirlwind day to tour the NICU, meet nurses and doctors, and most importantly, to talk with the surgeon. Courtney, the hospital's parent/hospital liaison coordinator (Program Manager is her official title), greeted us at the main office. I haven't met many people like Courtney—her kindness shone through and wrapped us up like a warm blanket. And at this point in our journey, we needed that compassion.

"Hi, Chris and Katie. It is so wonderful to meet you, and the team is really excited to get to know you. Here is a packet I prepared and some notebooks to take notes. Would you like anything to eat or drink?" I never wanted this woman to leave. *Is there a way for her to just take care of me through this all?* It was wishful thinking as we looked at our itinerary for a very busy day at the hospital.

The morning was a flurry of handshakes and faces. We met nurses, doctors, and specialists. We toured the floors of the hospital, making sure to spend the most time on the NICU floor. It was important to ask a few key questions: *When and how will I get to NICU from the Labor and Delivery floor? How many visitors can we have? How does the nurse schedule work? Will we have the same nurse every time?* And, most importantly, *when will I be able to hold my baby boy?*

Then we met one of the neonatologists, Dr. Cote, in a conference room. I didn't realize that so many different doctors work with fragile babies, so I had no idea what a neonatologist was. In my layperson words, the neonatologist is the doctor who does the day-to-day for the baby and coordinates all the moving parts of that care plan. The neonatologist therefore oversees all the specialists—the surgeon, the cardiologist, the pulmonologist, the urologist, the respiratory nurses, the NICU nurses—and makes sure that they are all communicating for the overall well-being of the baby. Dr. Cote was sharp as a tack, compassionate beyond my expectations, down to earth, and kind; I immediately fell in love with her. She was also close in age to me, a new mom, and nearly six feet tall like me. I felt yet another sign. I would learn later that she is also a phenomenal communicator and took the time to explain very complicated medical issues and procedures in comprehensible language. We wouldn't know yet how perfectly timed her presence and support in our son's birth would turn out to be.

After learning about all these moving parts, my head was spinning, but in a good way; I knew now that my baby's care would be fully covered.

Now, it was time to meet who I thought was the cornerstone of our care plan: the pediatric surgeon, Dr. Shapiro. I had researched him. I had asked a few of my (new) contacts at Emory University and Boston Children's Hospital about him, and everyone raved about him. He was a world-renowned pediatric surgeon with an impeccable reputation. I was so excited—and nervous—to meet him. My nerves were a little more on edge because he was our last meeting, and I was so tired, hungry, and overwhelmed with all the information we had just received. Fortunately, I had spent a lot of time in the past weeks coming up with questions for Dr. Shapiro, particularly about his surgical philosophy.

There are two main surgical philosophies for treating a baby with an omphalocele: "paint and wait" or "silo." The former is a more conservative approach in which the medical team "paints" the omphalocele, so skin grows around it, and then you "wait" until the baby/child is old enough for surgery to, well, put everything inside! This could mean waiting until he was two years old. The latter, the "silo," is a more aggressive approach in which a silo is put around the omphalocele right after birth, and over the course of days or weeks, the organs are slowly put into the body by gently pushing and pulling the abdomen. Once the organs are all inside, the surgeon closes the skin and tries to attach the muscles. But as muscles grow slower than skin, many times a patch will be placed to attach the muscles and then, when the child is older, the patch is removed, and the muscles are attached in a different surgery.

I was praying that Dr. Shapiro followed the more aggressive "silo" approach. From what I was learning anecdotally, the majority of omphalocele babies are "paint and wait." At that time, I didn't know if I would have the patience or fortitude to do the "wait" part of the process; I wanted to get all surgeries out of the way as soon as we could. It turned out that Dr. Shapiro preferred the aggressive surgical philosophy as well. Right away, we were on the same wavelength.

But I had one more question for him. It was something that really puzzled me. "Dr. Shapiro, you teach at New York University. You travel all around the world. Pardon me for being a snob—but why are you here when you could be in Boston, LA, Philadelphia, or New York City at the bigger children's hospitals?"

His response, "Katie, you told me you lived in New York, right?"

"Yes, for ten years."

"Well, can you ski on a Wednesday in New York City?"

"Ah. No, you can't."

I knew, at that instant, he was our man. Dr. Super-Star Shapiro was here, and therefore, we weren't budging. But, he added, "I am planning to do a teaching session in Israel within the first three weeks in January."

I quickly responded, "No, you can't. We are scheduled for the third Monday in January for our C-section. You have to be here." He laughed and our meeting ended. He thought I was kidding, but really, I would have run on the tarmac to stop that plane to Israel if I had to. Dr. Shapiro, one of the premier pediatric surgeons in the world, had to fix my baby.

All these people at WRPH—Courtney, Dr. Cote, Dr. Shapiro—were messing up my "plan." I had been convinced that we would be shipping up to Boston and working with the team at Boston Children's. But this care team was phenomenal: a medical dream team. They were brilliant, experienced, compassionate, and just the right fit for our little family.

His journey was ultimately going to be focused on releasing control, and here was a distinct moment I can look back on and see that I, for the first time, surrendered. This little boy, this journey, these people I was meeting were teaching me to stop, listen, and make decisions as they came. I wouldn't have picked this way to learn this lesson, but thank God it happened. This surrender wasn't a passive experience. Rather, it was a feeling that something bigger than my self-determination was leading me down this path toward people who knew what to do. And importantly, who was *I* to try to control it?

Being a controlling perfectionist wasn't (and isn't) sustainable. This, of course, was going to completely prepare me for motherhood: nothing is predictable with motherhood, no matter how hard you try to plan it all.

After the whirlwind day of meetings, Chris and I realized two important things: first and most importantly, this was our hospital and new home for a while. Boston was out. And second, we came to a place of acceptance that this was our new path. After the anger, shock, grief, and sadness (and a month of laying low from social engagements and our usual level of activity), this new phase of acceptance was finally accessible to me because I had the information and the support we needed to move along our new path.

I put my pregnancy books on the far corner of the shelf where they would collect a lot of dust. I now had the best resources, arguably in the world, just a phone call or email away. I started to live in the moment and didn't get too far ahead of things by worrying about breastfeeding or sleep schedules or what crap we needed to buy for a nursery. It was one of the first unique blessings of our journey. I truly didn't sweat about the small, stupid stuff and just focused on my love for this special baby boy. I wish more moms spent their pregnancies focused on just loving that little nugget growing inside of them instead of all the material things and the pressure to be perfect.

And from here on out, I made sure to stay away from Dr. Google.

CHAPTER 5

Baby Shower Bingo

By this point, I was about six months pregnant, and we fell into a groove, on cruise control. We came to a place of acceptance of our situation; we felt confident about all the members of our medical team, and our friends and family supported us in every way possible. I didn't obsess over the details of our little boy's birth or first weeks and months of life. I put it all in the doctors' hands and they were my proxy for God; I think that my trust and faith in the doctors were a form of prayer and gratitude to God. I didn't actively seek out God or talk to Him during this time. I continued my Hail Marys, but it was more a form of meditation to fall asleep. My spiritual life was on autopilot and that was okay. But no matter how I tried to go it alone, God was relentlessly pursuing my heart, putting the right people in my life, and giving me stamina and courage, even though I couldn't see it at the time.

Chris and I, during this stage, were excellent at avoiding the what-ifs, Google, and even social media. I joined an amazing, private Facebook group for parents of babies born with omphaloceles, but I was very careful about how much I looked at it. I wanted to know enough information to learn the proper vocabulary and to ask good questions. I also wanted to see and learn about the "success stories," but I simply could not read about the very extreme, medically complicated kids. And I could not read about the babies who died. I hope this doesn't sound insensitive, but at that stage of our journey, it was not a place I could go. So, I was careful about how much omphalocele content showed on my Facebook feed. I controlled my everyday environment, my digital world, my friend circle, and calmly got by, day by day.

Though I was stable, I did not fall into a blissful state of pregnancy as many do at this point in normal pregnancies. A few things reminded me of this. When a stranger would say, "Oh, how exciting to be having a baby," I would just nod my head. Or if someone mentioned a maternity photo shoot, I would bristle internally. The other thing I noticed was that I had no interest in having a baby shower, or even buying baby stuff. But I tried not to think about that too hard either.

And then one day the reality of the anger and fear I was holding in forced its way through during a routine shopping trip. I was in Target to buy face wash and wandered over to the baby section. I pulled out a onesie. And then I had a panic attack. My body froze, but it felt like my full belly dropped to the floor as if I was on a roller coaster. And then there was a dull *wump, wump, wump* sound in my ears, like an onset of sudden tinnitus. It lasted a minute or two—who knows how long I stood in the aisle staring blankly at the onesie— before my body and mind normalized and were back in sync. I left my basket with my face wash and ran out of the store. I was heaving with each breath and found a place to sit while tearfully dialing my mom in Massachusetts. "Mom, I just can't. I can't. I can't go near the baby stuff at Target. Mom, I just can't. I just can't. Why can't I buy my baby anything? I just can't." That's all I said, over and over again.

"So, don't," she replied. "Don't buy anything."

We spent the next fifteen minutes calming me down. I left the Target lot empty handed and sad. I kept trying to convince myself that many cultures think it is bad luck to buy items for a baby before it's born, but I knew that my feelings were deeper than superstition. While I had surrendered to my situation, I was still human. I still felt the grief and injustice of it all. Some part of me was still very, very not okay.

Surprisingly, that was the only true meltdown I had during the pregnancy until the final days leading up to my son's birth.

But the question of to-baby-shower or not-to-baby-shower wouldn't go away. I was more than halfway through the pregnancy, but I couldn't bring myself to have one, even though many friends were offering to host one. Though we were receiving positive updates, I had constant fear that my baby would be stillborn or that he wouldn't survive long after delivery. "I am following the Italian and Jewish customs that baby showers are bad luck—an invitation for something to go wrong," I liked to say. *How could I register for things that, at this time, felt so trivial? How could I happily attend and receive dozens of presents when my son's life felt like it hung in the balance?*

At the same time, there were other emotions bubbling under the surface that made everything feel chaotic. I felt angry that I was robbed of a normal pregnancy. I thought to myself, *I don't think I would even want a dumb shower with balloons and baby bingo and photo booths, but I wish I had the choice.* And instead of gently allowing the anger, I stifled it because I felt that if I were angry and stressed, the baby would get angry and stressed (which may be true). I didn't realize it at the time, but I was in a vicious feedback loop of anger with a chaser of self-judgment. I was mad at myself for being angry. And I was angry about being angry.

The battle of the baby shower raged on within me, sparking past feelings and kindling more self-judgment. I was still angry at my early arrogance of assuming I would have a normal pregnancy with a healthy baby in the first place. And now, I thought to myself, *Was it because of my arrogance and entitlement that I expected an easy, innocent pregnancy and healthy child that made me deserve this situation? Or was it because of my past actions that God was judging and punishing my unborn baby?* I think, whether it's through a religious frame or not, this a universal way of thinking about grief: we think we *did* something to cause our suffering, rather than things just happening beyond our realm of comprehension.

I was also really sad—sad, that I couldn't have a joyous pregnancy "like everyone else." Sadness is harder for me to handle than anger, so I tried to manage this part of my grief meticulously. I kept a subconscious scorecard of our trauma. In the bad column, we received a horrible ultrasound with news about our unhealthy baby and we had to perform an amnio on the spot. In the good column, we received good news from the anatomy scan and amnio results. And Dr. Shapiro gave us a positive forecast on our son's omphalocele repair. And that's how I lived—on the edge, trying to even out the balance of good and bad in my head, trying to keep the sadness from consuming me, even though I had zero control over it all. These were the first pangs of PTSD but, of course, I was living in it, so I was clueless that this elusive mental health issue was seeping into my core.

I look back and see that, of course, there was an emotional roller coaster of "I'm fine. I'm not fine. I'm really angry. I've surrendered. Oh wait—I'm sad again." I've now come to realize there is no playbook for grief. None. And that's why enduring grief is so hard, so individual, so personal.

And then a surprise blessing snapped me out of my agonizing self-analysis. One of my colleagues, Sharon in the Boston office, insisted that I have a baby shower when she and other team members visited the western regional office. I kept blowing off her suggestions of a traditional baby shower, until we finally settled on a great idea: a baby book shower! After all, we worked in publishing, and building my baby's library felt like the right and only thing that would fit his unordinary birth plan.

It was an unusually warm day in December. I bought a new maternity dress for the occasion. I felt nervous but also excited for the first time in a long time to be with my friends, who felt closer than just work colleagues. Sharon and Jennifer, another colleague, decorated a conference room, transforming the space from dull office gray into a bright burst of all the blues one could imagine.

I knew they were giving me a shower, but the surprise of seeing the office space metamorphosis and the whole office gathered together renewed my spirit. I was overwhelmed by their kindness and generosity. I gently wept, trying to wipe away the tears before they made a mascara mess on my face and new dress. *All of this, for me and the baby*, I thought to myself. *I'm blessed.* "Everyone, thank you," I stammered. "I am so grateful. I am just so touched. Overwhelmed . . ."

Sharon snapped me out of the sentimentality in typical New Englander style. "Jennifer, get her a cupcake. Ashley, get the first gift ready. And sit here at the head, Katie." Sharon's take-charge attitude and familiar accent had a deeply comforting effect on me: she reminded me of home—direct, deeply supportive, salt of the earth.

We gobbled cupcakes as I opened all the gifts. Each friend gifted me their favorite children's book for me to read to Tim in NICU. We laughed and talked, and I felt like myself.

Again, it wasn't how I planned it, but it was better than I imagined because reading to my baby would be an intimate way of bonding when I was unable to snuggle him in his first days and weeks of life. And the best part about my baby shower—I got to finally make a decision, and I decided no baby shower bingo.

After the shower, I continued on cruise control with work where I was having one of my best sales years to date. The stress of my personal situation gave me laser-like focus at work because I didn't want to think about how terrified I truly was. I also had doctor's appointments all the time. My manager, Mike, was wonderful, letting me take time to go to all my appointments. I would work in the reception area of the doctor's office, on the sonogram table, or while I waited for blood work. Some people demonize work, but as the old saying goes, "Idle hands are the devil's workshop." I would tweak that for my own experience: idle *minds* are the devil's workshop.

Paradoxically, life was a little boring now. Work, Chris, the high-risk practice appointments, and a handful of very empathic friends became my refuge. My world was smaller and quieter than my usual life, but I felt very stable with this state of affairs.

At the time, I wasn't in therapy, but I bet if I was, a therapist would say that at this time I was in the first stages of grief: shock. Although things seemed okay on the outside, underneath, they very much weren't. I know that denial often accompanies shock at this stage, but I don't think I was feeling denial. In fact, I think I was feeling the opposite of denial. Every day I was numbing, avoiding, distracting myself from three terrible thoughts: *What if Tim is stillborn, disabled, or in the NICU for a year?* These outcomes felt intolerable to me. I felt like I knew too much and was terrified that our outcome would be tragic.

CHAPTER 6

The Hail Mary

It was the end of November, and I was due the third week of January. This is the point, in most pregnancies, when women feel heightened fatigue and discomfort. I didn't feel these things. I was so fixated on my baby's health that I didn't think about my own health. In some ways, this was great. But in other ways, it was a bit foolish. I ran myself ragged in the last weeks of pregnancy. I didn't want to overthink things or indulge in myself because things were starting to get real.

Lisa and I were still working on our big deal, which hadn't closed yet. We had only a few weeks to close it and hit our sales goal. I felt the pressure of it, but it was an internal pressure. Sure, we had aggressive and high-achieving sales managers and leaders who wanted this deal to come in. And many on my team feared these leaders. But that was nothing to me. If nothing else, this difficult pregnancy journey taught me that the most important things in life were God, family, and health.

No. The real reason I was pushing myself so hard over this deal was to earn a significant bonus to pay for our medical bills. Chris and I had great jobs, well-to-do families, and lots of retirement savings, but I felt pressure to stock away a lot of money that we would have at our fingertips for our son's medical costs. I didn't stress out about financial matters on a daily basis. After all, as a bartender who also had a child with chronic health issues said to us when he heard our story, "Money problems aren't real problems. You can always make money." (Yes, we were at a bar, but I had a lemonade.) Or, as my dad said, "Money is fungible!"

I have dug deep in the years following to understand why I developed this deep-seated fear about money. *Was having a surplus of money just a security blanket? Was it that we were saving for a new house and the potential medical bills would derail this plan? Was it a way for me to transfer my real fear—of my son not surviving—onto something less scary, like a money problem? Or was it the recollection of a conversation with my dad, right after the omphalocele diagnosis?* "Katie, I don't want to scare you, but you may have to quit your job to care for this child. And this isn't just a year or two; he might need a full-time caretaker because he will be so fragile, and that caretaker will be you." I think the last part is what stuck in my head, even though I shoved it to the back until we got closer to the due date.

To this day, I'm not really sure why I became obsessed with finances. I suppose that's how fear and phobias work. They aren't grounded in reason or logic. And I had enough troubles on any day ending in Y, so why did I add this to the pile? I still don't know. But I was fixated on this bonus.

Our sales year ended in mid-December. As the days ticked by and the sale hadn't closed yet, I shifted from anxiety and anger to hopelessness. I fell into victim mode. *Of course this is happening. Of course we won't get the deal. Everything about this year has been a total disaster and this is just the cherry on top*, I quietly whined to God and to Chris.

In retrospect, I wish I had petitioned St. Paul and St. Timothy through all this. After all, Chris and I were inspired by St. Paul's letter to Timothy in which he wrote about courage over cowardice (2 Timothy 1:7). Why couldn't I apply this wise advice to myself as well as for a projection for my son? I wish I had turned that victim mentality into a victor one, but in those moments, I wasn't as spiritually strong as I am now, post-NICU, post-COVID, and post–other life trials.

I was open with Mike about the situation, and while he wanted the deal to come in, he never applied additional pressure on me. Mike was a special boss who was human and compassionate and didn't fixate on my business outcomes as much as my mental health and overall well-being. And as I suspected and later found out, our entire executive team for our business unit was very worried about me because they all knew what was going on. They wouldn't give me the bonus just because of my troubles, but they also laid off the heat they might have usually given someone trying to close a big deal. In that moment, I would have been upset to know that they treated me differently. Now, I am forever grateful for their compassion and empathy.

Lisa and I set up one more meeting in which I prepared one of the best and most elegant sales plans that I have ever written for her to present in person, as I could not fly at this point in the pregnancy. I spent hours on it, paring it down, taking complex ideas and making them very simple, until what started as a twenty-page document was reduced to one page, front and back, as the potential client preferred brevity. This was it: us two women from Holy Cross were heaving the Hail Mary pass.

And—it worked! We won the huge deal, in the eleventh hour. I remember that we got the verbal approval over the phone the afternoon of our year-end. I had to beg the client's secretary to stay an extra hour at work (Mountain Time is two hours behind Eastern Time in Philadelphia) so she could retrieve all the signatures and fax (fax, ugh!) the signed paperwork to us. It felt dramatic. It was dramatic. I remember I was wearing a cute purple and black, boatneck tunic dress with leggings, camped out in front of the fax machine at two thirty p.m. Mountain Time (which is four thirty Eastern Time) so I could report the signed contract to management by five p.m. Eastern Time in order for us to officially achieve our sales goal by the year-end deadline.

Mike was in his office. I ran-waddled over to his desk, clutching the signed contract as well as the fax receipt proving that it had been sent off to Boston, our company headquarters. "MIKE! THE CONTRACT CAME IN! LISA AND I DID IT!"

We made the deal. We both got the big bonus. And later, we were awarded a trip to Grand Cayman as part of the "President's Club" for excellence in sales. But most importantly, the intercession of Mother Mary provided for me and Lisa. Mary continued to be at my side even when life was on cruise control, when life got manic around the year-end and the holidays, and when I was so happy in my victory lap that I didn't even take time to thank her. None of that mattered; she nurtured, protected, and guided me in my hour of need, and she didn't need credit or recognition for it. And she wasn't done yet.

It turned out that a career in sales was ideal for having a January baby. The fiscal year for my company ended mid-December, and a new sales goal was set up at the beginning of the New Year. The big deal came in, I was able to have a nice and tidy wrap-up for the year, then and I shifted gears to "baby mode."

I suppose, though, that I was already in "baby mode" at this stage: I couldn't escape the big belly, the kicks inside the tummy, and the overall discomfort. And for me, with a high-risk pregnancy, I had countless appointments. Starting at week thirty-six, which coincided perfectly with the final days of our year-end, I had to go to the high-risk practice three times a week for "non-stress tests." Basically, the high-risk patient (me) is set up in a comfortable room and the nurses place a monitor around the belly to listen to baby and monitor the levels of amniotic fluid. Some may find these appointments and their frequency to be a pain in the butt, but I loved them. It brought me peace to know that my baby was being watched so carefully, and I enjoyed having the nurses dote on me. I was so hard-core with being focused during this pregnancy journey that I hadn't really allowed myself to be nurtured in the traditional sense—no pedicures, prenatal massages, or babymoons for me—but these visits and the care of the nurses allowed me to rest and receive their care.

It had been about two months since we did our tour and had spoken with the team at Western Regional Pediatric Hospital. I don't know where it came from, but I had this sudden and urgent need to meet with key members of our son's medical team to preview our plans for his care. My maternal instincts started to go into overdrive, and one night I said to Chris, "Wait, how long are we going to be in NICU?"

He replied, "You know—we never asked them that during our tour of the hospital."

I had to find out.

There is a joke about NICU: Ask a pediatric surgeon and a neonatologist how long a baby will be in NICU. The surgeon will reply, "A day." The neonatologist will respond, "A year." I don't think Dr. Shapiro *actually* said, "one day," but I recall that he implied the NICU time would be rather short. And I went with it. I needed that blissfully short NICU prediction to get through the pregnancy. But now? Now, I knew in my gut that there was no way we would have a short NICU stay. And I think I knew it all along because I was so driven by that sales bonus because *what if I had to quit my job to care for our son?* That bonus would keep us afloat for a while. I also recalled that conversation with my dad, very early on in the pregnancy, in which he compassionately told me to have a plan for leaving my job in case my son needed care that superseded what a nanny or day care could provide. This seed was planted early on, but it wasn't until the impending birth that it blossomed into a reality for me.

In short, the anxiety was real.

I called Courtney, the hospital coordinator, to set up another meeting with key members of the medical team. "Courtney, I know we didn't plan this, but I just need to talk with the team again. I'm not really sure who we should meet with but . . ."

I didn't need to say anything more. Courtney completely understood and set up a meeting the following week with Dr. Cote.

We met with Dr. Cote about three weeks before my C-section, which was scheduled for the third Monday in January. We sat down at the same conference table as before. I started the conversation.

"I know we met before, but it's getting so close. I don't have any specific questions, but, well, I know every baby is different, but is there any way you can estimate NICU time for our son?"

From all my research and my private omphalocele group on Facebook, I knew that no two babies are the same, nor can anyone accurately predict NICU time. Modern medicine can give us tons of information about the size of the omphalocele (six centimeters for our son), what's contained in the ompha- locele (liver and small and large intestines for our son), and if there are other affiliated conditions such as heart issues (none so far), but we wouldn't exactly know any further details un- til the baby is born. And we wouldn't know how the baby would tolerate surgery and recovery. There were so many un- knowns, and for a long time during the pregnancy, I avoided the uncertainty out of self-preservation. For me, this was the healthiest route. As I said before, if I let my mind spiral into the what-ifs and the depths of the unknown, I would have completely fallen apart.

But now it was time to explore the unknown as best we could. I didn't want to, but I knew we had to.

"I would expect to be here until the Fourth of July." Dr. Cote's statement struck me like a clap of thunder.

"Wait, wait, wait. He will be born in January. We will be here for *six months?* The *Fourth of July*?!"

I crumbled. But deep down, I wasn't shocked. I was shocked to actually hear it, but I wasn't shocked at the duration. This was major stuff—putting organs inside of a body. There were so many pieces to the puzzle of this massive recovery plan for such a tiny human.

Chris was stunned. We clutched each other's hands.

"That means our son will be in NICU for *six months?*" I was repeating myself, but I needed to make sure I got the math right.

"Yes. I would estimate six to nine months in NICU," she said.

Holy crap. Now, it's six to nine *months?*

Again, I was stunned. Being in NICU for nine months was like another pregnancy. I remember that when I found out the diagnosis way back in September, my initial thoughts were that we would be in the hospital for a long time. And I saw that many of the babies in my omphalocele Facebook group had longs stays in NICU. I buried all this information from the time we got the diagnosis until now. Living in self-chosen ignorance during the majority of the pregnancy was the right course of action for me and Chris, but we couldn't afford to be ignorant now; we needed to be prepared and courageous.

It was challenging to stay hopeful. This news, while not shocking, just added a layer of tough reality to the situation. Even though this was not the news we wanted, it was much, much better to hear it now, have a few weeks to process it, and navigate NICU with gusto and courage.

Fourth of July, I thought. *Crap.*

Christmas came and went quietly. We stayed locally, of course, and celebrated with Chris's family. Chris and I went to the Cathedral for Christmas Mass, but I didn't have a heart-to-heart with God or Mary during this time. The Cathedral was gorgeous, but I didn't feel moved by the ambiance or the homily; I was going through the motions. I wasn't angry at God or anything, I was just in a weird transition phase of wrapping up work and preparing to become a mom in a way that many can't fathom. But again, I wasn't angry—I think I was exhausted.

It feels strange to me now that I wasn't moved or inspired by the Advent season and Christmas. After all, the story of Jesus's birth is a beautiful, humble, and miraculous story.

Of course, to me, this world-changing event was the birth of the Messiah, but when you think of it from a simple mothering perspective, Mary had quite the series of trials: learning that she, a virgin, was carrying the Son of God; telling her new fiancé, Joseph, this extraordinary news; traveling ninety miles—on a donkey!—from Nazareth to Bethlehem while nine months pregnant because of the mandatory census by an oppressive government; and delivering a baby in a barn. And then, two years later, an angel visited Mary and Joseph to warn them to escape Egypt because King Herod wanted to kill the Israelite baby boys because he felt his power threatened.

On the verge of motherhood myself, why didn't I respond to her motherhood story? Why didn't I look to how she accepted her fate and quietly endured such difficult circumstances? All those months of praying to her and I never meditated on her difficult pregnancy and entrée into motherhood. Now, having been through the NICU experience, I feel the precious miracle of motherhood, especially Mary's, acutely.

January arrived.

My parents flew in from Boston the Saturday before the scheduled C-section on Monday. I was relieved to see them. They are a bustle of positive, joyful, and fun energy even in times of crisis. We planned a fun weekend before baby boy was to arrive. We had dinners planned, a party at our local beer garden, a manicure and pedicure . . . and the Broncos game.

"*Katie?*" Chris slowly and quietly called to me in the early evening on Saturday.

"Hey. What's up?"

"*So* . . . Dan . . . got Broncos tickets . . . *and* they are face value . . . *and* your dad wants to go too, even though he hates the Broncos . . . *and* I know it's far away but can we go to the game tomorrow?"

"YES! GO!"

I knew that once we had the baby, there would be no luxuries in our life for a while. Or, more that the guilt of such fun would be hard for us when our baby was in NICU.

"Chris, GO!"

So, they went to the Broncos game the day before our son was born. The Broncos lost. But that was a good thing because I am a die-hard Patriots fan, and the Pats were still in the playoffs. Even through my trials, I kept my priorities straight.

I used to travel a lot for my job in New York City. I often didn't look at the itinerary until the night before, or even the morning of, the trip. There are three major airports in the metro New York area, and many times I didn't even know which airport I was flying out of until I got in the cab. In all my years of travel, I only had one mishap from this lack of preparation: I booked a rental car at O'Hare instead of

Midway. This was so minor and easy to fix that I continued with my haphazard ways well beyond my travel days. It's a funny quirk I have because if you know me, you wouldn't think I could ever let myself be this disorganized.

I applied this method of preparation (or lack thereof) for my scheduled C-section. I packed a bag the night before and really didn't stress about the contents of the bag because we lived twenty minutes from the hospital, and if I forgot anything, Chris could go home for it. And second, we live in a major metropolitan area. There are stores. I don't get why people get all wound up about "packing the hospital bag." Even if I had had a normal pregnancy, I'm pretty sure I wouldn't have packed a bag and instead told Chris to go home and get me some stuff when everything settled down.

We had an eight a.m. C-section. I didn't even think about pre-operation procedures, so my plan was to leave our house at seven fifteen. So why was Chris setting the alarm for five fifteen? "Why are you setting it so freaking early?" I asked.

"Katie, did you read the instructions? We need there to be at six. This is *surgery* and they have to prep you for surgery."

It sounds naïve, but I really thought a C-section just happened. I knew recovery was hard, but I didn't think of the preparation ahead of time. Fortunately, I did listen to the part about not eating for twelve hours before the event. I followed those instructions and hadn't eaten since six p.m.

Another thing I hadn't prepared for was my anxiety. I did not sleep the night after we learned of the omphalocele diagnosis, but then I slept peacefully for the duration the pregnancy. But the night before our son's birth, I had difficulty falling to sleep. And the reason: I was terrified that our son would be stillborn. I was petrified, beyond reason, that I would not hear a cry when he was born. Now, he was safe in my tummy, protected in my iron-clad womb, with my laser-like focus and all the medical care he and I were receiving. *But out in this tough world, will he make it? If he does make it past birth, will his obstacles and challenges be so insurmountable that he won't survive the first hours or days of his life?* These thoughts tumbled over and over in my mind and translated into a lot of tossing and turning.

"Katie, what is going on? Why aren't you sleeping?"

"Chris, I can't tell you."

"Tell me."

"I'm afraid to say it out loud."

"Say it."

I started to sob. "Chris, I'm afraid he's going to die. I'm afraid he won't live."

"Stop. Don't even say it or think it!"

And he was right. I usually think that one shouldn't minimize someone else's thoughts or emotions and allow the person to feel their feelings. But there are times when a friend or family member needs to stop messing around by worrying about hurt feelings and say what needs to be said: I needed Chris to tell me to stop. I managed to sleep for only a few hours before the alarm went off.

It was time to get up and attend the birth of our son.

PART II

THE BIRTH AND NICU

CHAPTER 7

The C-Section

We left the house promptly at five thirty a.m. The ride from home to the hospital only took twenty minutes, and we had done this trip dozens of times because I had had so many appointments in the last month.

And yet, somehow, Chris took a wrong turn. Chris has one of the best senses of direction that I know. He could find his way out of anywhere, and he always pays careful attention to landmarks and road names. When he took the wrong turn, I knew he was just as scared as I was.

I find the stereotype to be true: if a woman tells a man that he's going the wrong way, he will get defensive, and a fight will ensue. We could not have a fight on this particular morning. I gently told him that he was heading in the wrong direction, and he replied, "Oh! Yes, you are right." And we got on the correct course. I was impressed at us for having such a calm reaction in a heightened moment.

We arrived at the hospital and checked in at the Labor & Delivery (L&D) desk. We were promptly ushered into our pre-op room. Again, I had been naïve in not thinking about the process of preparing for major surgery. I didn't realize until my second son was born, years later, how tense and controlled my firstborn son's birth really was. When PJ, my second son, was born, I walked into the pre-op room, music blared, the medical staff chattered about their weekends, and there was a looseness and feeling of routine (another day, another baby!) throughout the entire process.

Tim's delivery was way different. It was intense. I was poked and prodded. The tension led me to throw up a few times, even though I followed the directions about abstaining from food after six p.m. the evening prior. I believe I halfway fainted from all the nervous hustle and bustle, as I started talking gibberish and heard Chris say, "You can't get this woman to stop talking, even when she passes out." These small moments of levity were important to both of us when we were dealing with such a heavy situation.

"Okay, we are almost done and ready to start the C-section. One thing—you need to take off your necklaces," the nurse told me.

I had worn my Mary Medallion from the night we learned of the diagnosis, and I had never taken it off, not even to shower. Additionally, my mom had just given me a cherished necklace from my late grandmother, her mother, my Nana named Mary. When my Papa died back in 1997, Nana made his wedding ring into a heart necklace and never removed it until she passed away in early 2014. My mom kept it until this weekend, when she gave it to me to honor my new phase of life as a mother. I stacked the Nana Mary heart necklace with the Mary Medallion from my great-grandmother. I needed these necklaces, my Mary reminders, to get through my C-section. And I wasn't going to take them off.

"No, I won't take them off," I told her.

"No, you may not wear them. This is surgery and you cannot wear anything in the OR," said the assistant.

I was getting loopy, and the numbness from all the drugs was starting to course through my body so I couldn't protest in my usual fashion. I had to surrender to the moment, for the second time since I met the medical team at WRPH, and a sign of things to come. Just as I had to let go of my necklaces, I had to let go to the situation at hand which was the birth of my son. And like before, it was not a passive experience; there was courage in this surrender. I turned to Chris. "Chris, please make sure you put these in my purse and drop them to my mom as soon as you can. We can't lose these necklaces. I don't care about anything else."

Chris took his instructions seriously and clutched my purse to his chest. As I was wheeled into the OR, both sets of parents were waiting in the lobby. They saw us moving, and they jumped up to wish us well. The moment was actually quite funny. It felt like we were at the airport, and they were wishing us "bon voyage" as we headed off on a fabulous trip. They were so enthusiastic and excited. I had perhaps overlooked the fact that they were thrilled to have a grandson. I suppose we were going on a new adventure and, reflecting back on it, it was the right way to send us off: with positive vibes and enthusiasm. Now that I am a parent, I wonder if, internally, they were scared that their own babies—Chris and me— would have to endure such hardships in the next hours, days, weeks, and months, and they had to put on a brave, positive front just like we did for our son during my pregnancy.

Chris tossed the purse to my mom, and I saw her catch it. *Phew,* I thought. *My necklaces are safe.*

"C-sections are so fast. It takes, like, five minutes," someone told me.

This is a lie.

C-sections don't take five minutes. And they especially don't take five minutes when you allow a multitude of medical students to participate in your C-section. Chris and I had signed what seemed like a million waivers to allow medical students to witness our son's birth so they could learn more about delivering an omphalocele baby. It was another way to squeeze as much silver lining out of our experience as possible—contributing to the well-being of future babies with this birth defect.

The C-section was the weirdest feeling in the world. I could see and hear everything in the room. I opted to keep a screen up so I couldn't see the baby extracted from my womb. I couldn't feel anything from my neck down, yet I could sense the big movements. Chris was seated at my right. When I turned in that direction, not only did I see Chris, but I saw the giant digital clock hanging on the wall. As the minutes ticked by, I thought of that *C-sections take five minutes* statement that someone told me and started panicking. Five minutes had come and gone. We were moving onto minutes eight, nine, ten . . . twelve . . . fifteen . . . twenty.

Suddenly, I smelled Beautiful Perfume, by Estée Lauder, waft through the air. I immediately perked up. I swiveled my head in the other direction, my left, where the assistant to the anesthesiologist stood. I asked her, "Are you wearing Beautiful Perfume? The one by Estée Lauder?"

She replied, "Katie, no. You know we aren't allowed any perfumes or smells in the OR. It has to be fragrance-free and antiseptic in here."

And I started to weep. My Nana, Mary, who had passed away in early 2014, whose special heart-shaped necklace I inherited, wore Beautiful Perfume. This supernatural experience told me that she was there with me. *She was in the room with me! It was her!* It was her, here to comfort me because I was completely powerless to everything in this situation and still terrified that my baby would be delivered stillborn. I felt waves of peace in that moment. I didn't know if everything would be okay, but Nana was with me, and she was trying to tell me it would be okay, even if it wasn't. For the second time that day, I completely surrendered to the moment. My Nana, from heaven, was with me in the OR.

Then, I heard it. In the thirty-fourth minute: the cry. My baby boy was wailing. I exhaled a huge sigh of relief. *He's crying, he's crying, he's crying!* It was a wonderful sound, that cry. The cry of life.

Choking on my own sobs, I told Chris to leave my side and go with our baby boy. During our hospital tours and interviews with the doctors and nurses, the medical team had prepared me that there was a 90 percent chance that I would not be able to see or hold my baby after delivery because he would have to go to surgery immediately. So, we planned that Chris would go with the baby after birth, travel down the long hallways with our son to bring him to surgery; he even did a test run of the hallways during one of our visits. I would stay back and be taken to recovery. Many cannot believe that this was the plan and felt pity for me that I would not be able to see or hold my baby, but I didn't feel that way at all. It was my first test of motherhood—this wasn't about *me*; it was about my baby. If my baby needed surgery, he had to go. I would see him when it was the proper time. I had to do what was best for my son, not what was best for me.

But things changed.

A redheaded, slimy newborn was placed on my chest. I rarely say that things are surreal, but this was surreal. Tears were streaming down my face. I was so happy and relieved. And I looked up at Chris and stammered, "Chris . . . he . . . he . . . he . . ." I looked back down at my newborn son. "He has the biggest ears I have ever seen!" In fact, he looked like an alien.

And then, minutes later, our newborn son, Timothy Simons McCarty, with his big ears, was whisked away for surgery.

I still can't believe that my first reaction to seeing Tim was that he was slimy, had big ears, and looked like an alien. But I was so happy because humor, like work, is a way for me to navigate serious and difficult situations: the perfect antidote to anxiety. And it was finally time to laugh. *Finally*! When I had a funny reaction, like to Tim's initial appearance, I knew God was telling me, "Katie, everything is okay."

I also knew God was there because, as I was being wheeled away to recovery, there was more humor. There were a few medical students exiting with me. One of them was a strapping, tall, handsome man. My doctor, Dr. Taylor, was also with him. Dr. Taylor was a young, beautiful doctor with perfect hair and porcelain skin. I looked over to the medical student and said, "You are the hottest doctor ever. I bet you do CrossFit." I continued, "And Dr. Taylor, you are the most gorgeous woman in the world. You guys need a show."

They exploded into laughter. Here was this serious, tense, dramatic moment, and we were all in stitches. I couldn't feel anything, but my face hurt from all the smiling, laughter, and tears of joy. Now that I reflect, I can't recall much laughter while I was pregnant. But now, my son, Timothy, the little, redheaded alien with giant ears, was born! Hallelujah! And he was a busy little guy, already off to an afternoon of "meetings" with important people.

Dr. Shapiro and the medical team were now going to evaluate the size and contents of the omphalocele and determine if Tim could tolerate a surgery in which his organs were put into his body. It turned out that Tim had a *giant* omphalocele (the actual medical term). Once Tim was born, the doctors had to decide when to put all the organs inside his body: right away or over time. The latter would have to happen if his abdominal cavity was too small. In that situation, Dr. Shapiro would place a "silo" around the exterior organs and, over the course of days or weeks, stretch his abdominal cavity and push the organs inside the body.

Either way, our little dude was having major surgery ("everything in" or silo surgery) within hours of his birth. I knew all of this ahead of time, and I am forever grateful that I was loopy, recovering from the drugs of the C-section, and so didn't have to deal with the details of his surgery and sign consent forms. It was Chris who stayed with Tim for all his pre-surgery procedures, absorbed all the critical information, and made the decisions. Chris held it together while he had a wife in recovery and a son who was having tubes and wires shoved down his throat, a central line put in his tiny chest, and scurried off to surgery. Chris was a hero in those moments, and I was grateful to him.

While all of this was happening, I was brought to the recovery area and was sipping on ice chips, all by myself. The silence and solitude of the moment were exactly what I needed. I needed some time to collect myself, to enjoy this moment, to breath a huge sigh of relief that my primary, biggest fear hadn't come true: Tim was alive. He was born at seven pounds, eleven ounces—big enough to tolerate surgery.

We had prepared for Tim's impending surgery, but I didn't know what was going to happen to me now. After enjoying some minutes of peace to myself, I thought: *Wait, now what?*

My dad and sister-in-law, Jennifer, popped their heads behind the curtains. They are both gentle and quiet people, so they were the right ones to visit me in that moment. There weren't high fives or pep talks; instead, they quietly asked me how I was doing. When they both stepped out a bit later, I again relaxed into the solitary, peaceful joy of the moment. Some victories have to be celebrated alone.

CHAPTER 8

The Baby Without Wires

I delivered Tim on the third Monday of January at 8:34 a.m. About three hours after his birth, the surgeons decided the omphalocele was too big to put everything in all at once. So they did silo surgery. I have pictures of me on the NICU floor, visiting Tim sometime during the day of his birth, probably before his surgery, but I can't remember being there; it was likely all the pain medication made me forget the many hours following his birth. I may not remember, but I have pictures: Tim's tiny fingers and my finger entwined.

Once Tim was away and the C-section was complete, I was brought to the maternity floor and had a fleet of nurses doting on me. I thought to myself, *This is pretty sweet! Maybe they do this for all high-risk moms who are going through the ringer and have to deal with NICU.* It was so nice, but it also felt weird. I am someone who likes attention, for sure, but I'm not a high-maintenance diva who needs a team of people to take care of me.

So, I asked one of the L&D nurses, "I love all this attention. But I'm starting to get a celebrity complex. You know, like those celebrities who have a baby and get an entire floor to themselves? Why am I getting so much attention?"

The nurse laughed. "You are too funny. Well, you are the only mom to deliver a baby today. So, you *are* the only one on the floor."

I didn't realize what a gift this was until the following day when the floor was filled to capacity. And it's not because I missed the attention; I heard all the babies. I was so naïve (yet prepared, for my own NICU mom journey) that I didn't realize that the newborn babies stayed in the same rooms as their mothers right after birth. I thought it was still like the old movies in which the babies were lined up, row upon row, in the nursery and would stay there while the moms rested until they were discharged. And after having my second baby, who was healthy, the memory of that image came back to me, and I wished they had a nursery for him! But that night, I heard the babies crying in the rooms. It was hard to hear healthy babies and their exuberant parents as they bumbled through their first night together, while Chris and I were alone in our tiny maternity room without Tim. I rarely felt jealousy during my pregnancy, but that night I felt the sharp pains of envy as acutely as the throbs from my C-section.

And it got worse.

The following day, I was encouraged to walk the floor to get my body moving and start my own recovery process. I was slowly doing my first lap around the floor, clinging to my IV pole, when a woman yelled out to me, "Katie, is that you?"

I looked behind me and saw a glowing new mom pushing a little bassinet without an IV pole. I had no idea who she was. I replied, "Yes. This is Katie. I'm so sorry—I forget your name." I also had *no* idea how this woman knew me, but I didn't mention that part.

"It's Jessica, from the Baby 101 class. How are you? How are you feeling?" I still had no idea who this woman was, but I didn't want to be rude.

She quickly caught up to me. And that's when I saw her baby—the baby without wires. Jessica was pushing a bassinet with a perfect little girl. The baby had on one of those little hospital-issued bows. She was sleeping soundly, and you could see her perfect little nose and tiny heart-shaped mouth. It was a peaceful, serene moment.

"I'm good. Um, yeah. I had a C-section, so it's slow-going. Wow! She is gorgeous. Congratulations. What is her name?"

Jessica replied, "She's Vivian, and we're going to call her Vivi. Thank you so much."

I don't remember the rest of the conversation, but I know that I was fascinated by this perfect creature and that I was gracious in the moment. I also know that Jessica never asked where my baby was. I shuffled back to my room, not completing my loop, and lost it.

I sobbed and sobbed and sobbed. *That was it? That was all? You had a baby after an innocent pregnancy. And you delivered your baby as naturally as you could so that you could easily complete a lap around the maternity floor, pushing a bassinet? And then, your newborn baby lies next to you at night? And you have a baby without any tubes or wires all over her body so that you can actually see her beautiful face? And you don't have to be wheeled nearly a mile to other side of the hospital just to see your baby in NICU?* I was in shock. The combination of jealousy, naïveté, hormones, and pain medication collapsed me into a crumpled mess on my hospital bed.

A nurse came in. She didn't even ask if I was okay; it was obvious that I wasn't. "Let it all out. Let it all out. Let it *all* out," she repeated as she held me. Big, huge, ugly tears were streaming down my face. They wouldn't stop, even though the sobbing hurt my weak abdomen that was still throbbing from the C-section. "Keep crying. Get it out."

I started to talk. "I . . . just . . . these babies . . . they don't have *wires* . . . You can see their faces . . . They don't have *tubes*," I said as my body heaved in her arms. "Is that all they have to do? Just have a baby and go home?"

The nurse responded, "Yes. You are right—they have the baby and go home. It's not fair. And I'm so sorry that you can't have that experience."

I was so relieved she wasn't an optimism bully.

She continued, "You NICU moms are heroes. You have the most difficult recoveries. You can't be with your babies. You travel across the hospital to visit with your babies. And you all . . . you . . . you . . . YOU NEVER COMPLAIN. You always say thank you and smile. Regular moms demand us to do all their crap, and they aren't happy with anything. 'The food here sucks.' 'I want the lactation consultant NOW because I have to have everything natural, and I must breastfeed immediately.' 'I stated in my birth plan that I wanted to have Enya playing in the background during my delivery, and no one put it on. I need to talk with someone.' I wish they could live a day in your shoes."

I appreciated her words so much, but I didn't want to be consoled like that. I wanted to be the tough, strong workaholic that I was during my pregnancy. I didn't want pity or to be the NICU martyr mom. I wanted to be happy for others. *Why was I crying like this? Why was I having these feelings? Jessica didn't do anything wrong, but why did she induce such a reaction in me?*

I responded as such. "I don't want to be this person. I don't want to be jealous and bitter. I want people to have beautiful babies. I just . . . I just . . ."

And the nurse stopped me. "You are human. Please be gentle with yourself right now." She stayed in the room with me for over an hour, just holding me until Chris came back from NICU.

It's hard to describe the compassion of strangers in these moments of darkness. That nurse was my light that night. And she didn't keep her goodness hidden so as not to pry into my life. She was my beacon of encouragement and kindness during a dark moment. During pregnancy, I was rather isolated and leaned on a fairly routine prayer life. But within hours of hospital life, that routine was thrown out the window. Now, God had to be present to me in a different form: He used strangers as His mouthpiece.

At the time, such a complete one-eighty from the joy after Tim was born to the grief a mere twenty-four hours later felt like such a setback. After all, I spent months trying to behave well so I could achieve a good outcome for me and my son. I thought virtuous behavior—mostly through self-control— would prove to God that I was worthy of a good outcome and an end to my trials. That God would deliver me from uncomfortable situations like what had just happened to me. That seemed just to me. *Isn't God supposed to be just? And if He's just, then He is good. So, if He is so good, why can't he make all these hardships, even the little ones, just stop?*

But that's not how life is. And it's not how God works. God is not a genie in the sky who grants us our wishes or a cosmic

Santa Claus showering us with gifts so that we are perpetually happy and never have problems. No. God is greater than this. And we simply can't understand His ways because we don't have His infinite perspective on our lives and the lives of everyone and everything in the universe.

I still don't know the ways of God, but I do know that in my own life, my hard times, such as this encounter, made me more vulnerable and turn to Him. And in doing so, God has transformed my character and my heart. Do I like experiencing grief and hardship? Heck no! But hardship will happen in everyone's life. It's inevitable; and it's also naïve to think hard times won't happen. So, how should one cope? I can't answer that. But for me, perfect, virtuous behavior was exhausting and didn't work anyway. It felt more honest to cry.

The next day, the hospital sent a financial guy into our room to explain payment policies for our difficult situation. I kicked him out of the room right away. I did not need to deal with this dude in my highly medicated state, nor did I want to conjure the fears about finances that I had had during the pregnancy. *Screw the finances! Who cares? We will go bankrupt if we must! The only thing that matters is that Tim lives.*

It turns out that bartender we met during my pregnancy was totally right: "Money problems aren't real problems. The only thing that matters is health." (We later gave feedback to the hospital that while it is helpful to have a financial planner visit with a NICU family, please wait at least a week or two until things have stabilized from the chaos of placing a baby in NICU.)

All the while, Tim was recovering from his silo surgery, and I went to NICU to see him recovering as much as I could. Even though it was difficult in our hospital to travel all the way from the maternity floor to the NICU, the NICU was my refuge from the maternity floor with all the healthy babies and the happy moms. I quickly realized that I had to be in an environment where there were more moms "like me," which is why the NICU floor became my sanctuary. It was harder now to discipline my emotions than when I was pregnant; the hormones and pain medication were no joke and toyed with my emotional equilibrium.

And of course, I wanted to be with Tim, my newborn son, but being with Tim was not easy. It was hard to recover from my own surgery and make the long trip to the NICU. And seeing Tim covered in the tubes and wires with the soundtrack of the constant whirring and humming of machines was sensory overload that had me in internal meltdown in the first days of NICU. I had to constantly remind myself that my precious baby boy, Timothy, was born. And his prognosis at birth—and not just hopeful predictions while he was still in my belly—was better than we could have ever expected. The best-case scenario was happening in real time. Tim was born full-term. He was strong enough to tolerate silo surgery, and he was stable after the surgery. But I was not okay.

I felt that Chris was connected to Tim through their post-birth experience, rushing off to surgery together. Chris also knew the NICU doctors and nurses right away because I insisted that he spend time in NICU instead of with me. I wasn't jealous of Chris—this was the best course of action, and Tim needed his daddy—but, at this point, I felt discon-nected from the entire motherhood experience.

I didn't have any emotions attached to this feeling of being disconnected. It wasn't anger, it wasn't sadness, it wasn't even jealousy. I just felt empty. I've never experienced true depres-sion, just the occasional blues. So, maybe I was teetering on the edge of depression those first few days. And I couldn't figure out what was making me feel so numb. I couldn't feel my heart.

Whatever it was, I continued to take my magical Percocet to help offset the C-section pain—which dulled my senses and gave me false comfort—and shuffled down the long hall-ways and through endless doors to NICU to see Tim, my baby with wires.

CHAPTER 9

Gridiron Abs

Over the course of the next few days, Tim's organs were slowly pushed into his abdomen via the silo, and he tolerated it beautifully with no stress to his lungs, which can be a common issue in his situation. As the organs are pushed into the body, they can push the lungs and cause respiratory issues. We were still waiting to see how long it would take to have all the organs put into the body. Then they would do the "closure" surgery.

All the while, I was adjusting to my new life in NICU. At first, NICU is terrifying. There are machines everywhere. There are beeps and blips, purring and whirring of a respiratory machine, the constant hum of thousands of watts of electricity for machines keeping babies alive. Nurses, doctors, respiratory specialists, janitors, counselors, and volunteers are constantly in and out of the small room, limiting private time for bonding. The baby is hooked up to endless tubes and wires and IVs and a breathing machine.

Tim was swollen from all the pain medication he had to take after his silo surgery. I joked that he looked like an alien when he was first born, but all newborns look that way. After they clean up, they are beautiful. Of course, Tim was beautiful too, but it was hard to see him—the real him—underneath all the tubes and wires. And his post-surgery puffiness, which made him look like he might pop like a balloon, often set me over the edge, reducing me to tears and storming out of that little, buzzing room, which then induced guilt in me. *How can I storm out of the room when he needs me for comfort and reassurance?*

Because Tim's tiny body was so fragile, Chris and I were not allowed to hold him during all this time. We participated in "care times"—scheduled time throughout the day in which we could wipe his eyes, change an occasional diaper, and touch his head and feet, but we could not free him from his tubes and wires and snuggle him. When people hear that I didn't hold my newborn after he was born, they are in shock. And yes, their reaction to my situation is accurate. My body and soul craved that bonding, through touch, but my head forced those feelings down. *You will have a lifetime of snuggles, Katie. Just be patient*, I told myself.

But at my core, I was unconvinced. I was enraged that I couldn't bond with my baby. *Am I afraid?* I'd ask myself as I stared at him through the plastic bassinet. *Am I afraid to get attached to him and then . . . what if he doesn't make it?*

I couldn't pinpoint the emotions—rage or fear or both—but I know that in those initial days, I stuffed them down, with the help of Percocet, so I felt numb and disconnected. (I am fortunate to report that this period of emptiness and depression was brief and that I didn't take more than a week's worth of the opioids that were prescribed for my C-section.)

After having my second son, PJ, who was born healthy and I was able to hold and snuggle him moments after his birth, I now know that the instinct to hold one's baby is primal. And I look back, and I want to hug the NICU-mama-me because her instincts were right: it's not natural to stare at your baby who is intubated and unable to move and not even give them a hug.

I knew something was off, but because Tim was my first baby, I didn't know how very off things were.

To add to this distress, I knew I would be leaving the hospital without my baby. I was mentally preparing to leave the hospital without Tim because our medical team predicted his long NICU stay, but it wasn't until we were filling out my discharge papers that it hit me: I'm leaving the hospital without my baby. The hospital required that all new parents do a crash course in bringing the baby home and what to expect in the first days and weeks at home. It didn't hit me until I was sitting at the table with the other parents and their babies that it wasn't a good idea that Chris and I attend. *Why am I sitting in this meeting when I'm not bringing home my baby? Why is this happening to me?*

I stifled my anger by presenting a brave yet sweet front. Chris and I introduced ourselves to the group and briefly told the group that our baby needed some time in NICU—no further explanation or detail because, if I elaborated, I would have lost it. A mom reached across to me, sensing my simultaneous grief and anger, grabbed my arm and kindly said, "I am a NICU nurse at this hospital. I just had my baby, but if I were down in NICU, I would be loving your baby like he was my own. You are in the best place with the best doctors and nurses anywhere. Please, believe me." I somehow held back my tears. What a coincidence that a NICU nurse was in my discharge class. Moments like these would happen a lot in NICU—profound grief and anger soothed, calmed, or even extinguished by the kindness, goodness, and authenticity of others. And it was in those tender moments that I knew that God was with me. With us.

There was another mom in the group without her baby. Like me, she didn't explain to the group what her situation was, but I immediately felt a bond with her. It was the first time that I realized that I wasn't a "normal" mom and felt drawn to others who were experiencing the same brokenness that I felt.

After the crash course that felt like an eternity, I was discharged from the hospital, and Chris and I went home without Tim.

We went home, and I began this strange maternity leave, a maternity leave that I never envisioned, a maternity leave without a baby. It did not seem wise to leave my job until we knew exactly what we were facing. It seems strange to me now that I didn't think through the logistics of maternity leave, especially since I had been meticulous about so many other details of this unordinary birth. I planned to take my twelve-week maternity leave in full, consecutively. But once I was actually in NICU, it was suggested that I break up the twelve weeks. For example, I could take four weeks to recover from C-section surgery and be there for the first important weeks of NICU. Then, go back to work and use the final eight weeks of maternity leave when Tim came home from NICU—whenever that was. As one doctor joked, "This is the best and most expensive day care you'll ever have!"

Chris and I were trying to figure out a groove in which we went to the hospital every day. I made sure to get showered and dressed every day, and I wore my sharp maternity work clothes. This process was very important to me because being put together on the outside helped to set the tone for all the internal challenges and rollercoaster of emotions that I was experiencing on the inside. And it made me think of Lisa: Lisa was always dressed up and poised. I wanted to be like that as I went through my own trials.

The pregnancy was challenging but controlled. But now? After Tim's birth, my feelings changed as often as the New England weather in spring. One minute, I was scared. The next minute, I was happy. Then an hour later, I was jealous. I was bewildered by all these conflicting emotions that overcame me so quickly. I thought that if I was put together on the outside, maybe I would feel better inside. I was willing to try anything.

In retrospect, I wish I turned to a more spiritual realm for comfort. I wish I had turned to the Beatitudes, though they can seem paradoxical! "Blessed are those who mourn, for they will be comforted," says Jesus in Matthew 5:4. I'm not sure I would have known how to process that bold statement during my trials, but now I understand it. At the time, I didn't let myself mourn; if I had, I would have been comforted. I think I didn't make myself vulnerable so that people could comfort me. People tried, but I put up walls so they would think I was handling things.

I also wish I had given into my feelings of homesickness. I was fifteen hundred miles from my friends and family back East. My parents had to leave days after Tim's birth, and I felt sad to see them go home. I also missed my siblings and sister-in-law—Lizzie, Andrew, and Sara. They were wonderful about texting, calling, and FaceTiming, but it wasn't the same. My siblings are also the funniest people I know, so I preemptively missed their quick jokes and sensitive levity to my heavy situation.

It turned out that my sister, Lizzie, was on a comedy TV show during our time in NICU, and when her face flashed on the TV screen, I experienced simultaneous pride and sadness. I didn't want her on a TV screen, I wanted her at my side. But we knew a visit to us at this point wasn't worth it because of the strict NICU visitor policy and our unpredictable schedule. Still, practicality isn't what the heart wants.

Dr. Shapiro and the team decided that they would be able to put all his organs inside his little body, attach his muscles with a Gore-Tex patch, and do "skin closure" one week after the initial silo placement. It was faster than we had expected. We thought the skin closure would happen weeks—not just *one* week—after his birth. It was unthinkable our son was already going to have his second surgery and he was only a week old. And we didn't have the mental bandwidth to prepare for how serious this surgery was, which was probably a good thing.

It was during his preparation for surgery that we finally felt the gravitas of the situation because we were allowed a significant moment: I was finally able to hold Tim. My son was a week old, but I hadn't cradled in my arms. Jill, our primary NICU nurse, superseded the doctors to take a detour in the surgery prep to let Chris and me hold Tim. The gesture took me by surprise for a few reasons. It's instinctual to hold one's baby, yet I was terrified to hold my fragile baby and had to be reassured by the nurse that I could do it. But deeper down, I was terrified to hold him because I feared it would be my first and last time holding my son. Jill removed all the tubes and wires and gently positioned Tim into my arms. It was the first time I felt connected to him outside of my tummy.

I was overwhelmed by our embrace and didn't want to let go of him. My tears fell gently on his face, and I tenderly wiped them away. I finally felt the bond that mothers feel. And I was scared because it was temporary. Now he had to go off to his second major surgery a week after his birth. It's hard for many mothers to understand, but many NICU moms can relate to how scared I was to get attached to him.

However, I knew in my gut that he would be okay, unlike my fears on the eve of his birth. In retrospect, it was a huge, risky, major surgery, and Chris and I should have been a lot more scared. Sometimes ignorance is such a blessing. We decided to go to lunch with Chris's parents and with one of my best friends from elementary school from Massachusetts,

Cara, who had moved out West years ago. We had a normal lunch and didn't talk about the surgery looming over us in the background.

The phone rang while we were at lunch: Tim was out of surgery. It was a success!

When I step back to reflect on this medical process, I now realize what a healing miracle this was: that modern medicine can reverse and heal this exceptional physical defect. Like the healing miracles in the New Testament, Tim's surgery (and subsequent surgeries) was a miracle.

Years later, when the family was playing Bible Scavenger Hunt (a game I invented) to share their favorite miracle, my second son PJ breathlessly told me, "My favorite miracle is when Jesus heals the little girl. I saw it on the video at school. You know the one. Where the daddy is running to Jesus so he can heal his daughter who will die. Mommy, she didn't die. And it's because the daddy ran fast to Jesus, and Jesus came and made her live!" His immediate and innocent retelling of this Bible story nearly made me weep as I realized that, like Jairus, the "daddy" in the Bible story, I ran toward Jesus to heal my own son.

We rushed out of the restaurant and beelined to the hospital. Chris and I went into his room and saw Tim in his isolette. To anyone other than a NICU mom, his appearance would have been a frightful sight. But I felt intense pride at the sight of these scars, which had a Frankenstein-like resemblance. The skin was pulled tight, held together with sutures, and the skin puckered.

Dr. Shapiro gave us a summary of the surgery. Tim had a strong heart and lungs and was able to tolerate surgery well. He added, "And I tried to create a bellybutton. We won't know if it stays until after he heals, but I tried to make one." That's an interesting fun fact about people born with omphaloceles: they don't have bellybuttons!

Dr. Shapiro tore off the bandage, and a blotch of thick, dark-red blood trickled down his tummy. "I did that for effect. He looks even tougher now." I nodded proudly. That image of Tim summed up a lot of what NICU is all about—intense, grotesque scars that represent strength. But my second reaction was alarm. *Such a big moment, but there's no way we can post these pictures on Facebook.* I reprimanded myself for having such an immature reaction to such a positive moment (and how social media, at that time, dominated a lot of my life). Yet, I felt that no one wants to see the process of surviving—because it's hard to look at. They just want to see the end result, which is pretty. And my gut instinct was correct. When I shared Tim's post-surgery pictures to a few, close family members and friends, I cried when a friend remarked, "Please put those away. It's too much."

In the NICU, I turned to humor—my preferred coping mechanism. "Oh my gosh, Chris, he has a football tummy! It looks like a freaking football!" I exclaimed. His stomach had ballooning quality—plus the row of thick, black sutures on top to keep the skin attached. The sutures looked just like the stitches on footballs. Then, I panicked. "Will it even out? Will the swelling and puckering go down?"

One of the doctors in the room, who knew I was a Patriots fan, replied, "Yes. It's a Tom Brady tummy. Don't worry. The swelling will go down. It will be your very own Deflategate," referring to the controversy that Tom Brady was deflating footballs to gain an advantage during playoff games.

It was a nice moment of levity, which I interpreted as good news because no one would joke if things were going badly. For once I had a thought that felt normal: *My goodness, Broncos fans are as annoying as Giants fans.*

CHAPTER 10
A Shoulder to Lean On

NICU families mark the days in numbers. After the skin closure, Tim's health stabilized from days eight through seventeen in NICU. After day seventeen, it wasn't quite the cruise control that I experienced during my pregnancy, but for the most part, Chris and I adjusted to the rhythm and routine of hospital life, although Tim was still in Level 4—the most acute level of care.

Chris and I realized an odd thing: we still hadn't heard Tim cry or utter sweet baby coos because he was intubated. That huge breathing tube not only covered his beautiful face, it made him mute. Most new parents complain about the endless cries of their baby. We hadn't heard our sweet baby boy cry since the minute he was born.

Tim was extubated on day seventeen in NICU, and I was scared he wouldn't have a voice. It was an irrational fear, and the nurses tried to convince me that his vocal cords would gain strength. But I was fast-forwarding to later in his life, and the thought that he would never speak scared me. In my overly verbal world, this seemed like a legitimate fear, but it was unfounded—after only a few days, he was wailing as if it was his native language. Finally there was a soundtrack to our NICU story. These little victories kept the days of NICU bearable.

After Tim was extubated, the medical team suggested that I try to breastfeed him. Since I hadn't been able to breastfeed so far, I was pumping around the clock but producing very little breast milk. I received advice to look at pictures of my baby to stimulate more milk, but it felt like a creepy form of masturbation. The whole breastfeeding experience, for me, was exhausting and demoralizing; I wouldn't have minded pumping or relying solely on formula—what I hated was not having a choice. One of the most primal and universal ways to nurture and bond with a baby is through feeding that baby, and the inability of many NICU moms to breastfeed is a major point of grief.

I was assigned a lactation consultant so that I could try breastfeeding now that Tim was extubated. Maybe breastfeeding would stimulate more success than pumping had? I was open to it! Mary, our lactation consultant, bustled into the room like a freight train. It was unsettling because everything is calm and contained on the Level 4 NICU floor. Mary was large and in charge, which is usually the type of woman I like and trust, but for some reason, in this environment, her presence immediately didn't fit. She burst into the tiny NICU room, and her Texan accent sounded foreign to my Yankee ears.

"Hi, Katie! I'm Mary, your lactation consultant! We are going to make this a positive experience for you and baby! Are you ready for this? It's going to be GREAT!" she boomed.

Oh goodness, I thought, breathing deeply. I am a high-energy, loud person, but this lady felt like a caricature, and I had to hold myself back from rolling my eyes.

Instead, I said, "Yep. I'm ready."

She had me remove my shirt and then manhandled my left breast. I was holding Tim in my right arm and she shoved him into my left boob. "See! You have to get him over there and gently guide his mouth to your nipple and HE WILL LOVE IT. See that? Breastfeeding is so IMPORTANT for Mama and baby. It's how you BOND. See? How will you BOND, otherwise? It's the BEST. It's so NATURAL." But there was *nothing* natural about this process: how she was smashing Tim's tiny face into my deflated breast, how she was spouting lame platitudes, how frantic it all felt. He was wailing and wailing, and I was scared I was suffocating the poor kid.

This went on for a solid five minutes—readjusting my boobs, pushing Tim into them, massaging his mouth, moving my boobs more, all the while, peppering comments like, "See, see, see? It should be FUN for you both. It will BOND you. And he will get all your IMMUNITIES. This is so important. He needs your IMMUNITIES. Get 'em, Tim! That's his name, right? Get the immunities from Mama."

While nothing about Mary felt comforting to me, her over-the-top manner turned out to be a blessing, the significance of her name growing by the hour: Mother Mary. She manhandled my boobs, shoving his tiny mouth onto them, and spouted off Southern sayings. She was so comical that my grief about my failure to breastfeed was replaced with joy. I was laughing for the first time in weeks. I know Tim felt that joy and laughter, and it was an alternative way to bond with him. As I was learning on my NICU path, the ways of loving, nurturing, and bonding are just different for NICU parents. And so is breastfeeding.

Which wasn't working.

So long breastfeeding, I thought. Tim and I (and Chris!) can bond over a bottle. That's why brilliant people developed formula so that babies didn't have to starve. And so Tim became a formula baby, and I felt zero guilt. Years later, when I was finally able to breastfeed my second son, PJ, I had a wonderful experience. So, I've come to understand that every mom, every baby, and every situation is different, and

I'm always careful to never judge what someone decides to do. NICU takes away the choice, which is maybe the hardest part about it.

Overall, NICU is serious stuff. Many throw around the acronym without stopping to realize the gravity of it: the IC stands for *intensive care*. Of course, I understood the literal meaning of *intensive care,* but it wasn't until I had a baby in intensive care that I really grasped the fact that these babies are in critical condition or are very ill. Some are teetering on the brink of death. Life feels contained and methodical, yet simultaneously out of control. That's why the experience is so different from what most parents and babies experience and why many can't understand how serious and scary it is.

NICU gave me tremendous perspective. Tim was a little shy of one month old and had already endured two major surgeries. I was thirty-seven years old at the time, and my first surgery *ever* was the C-section I had just had. And surgeries like these were happening in each and every room of NICU for dozens of families like ours. Tiny humans fighting for their lives, enduring surgeries or situations that most of us will never face in our lives.

I was learning that being in NICU was many times more emotionally turbulent than I could have predicted. During pregnancy, it felt necessary to stay strong and focused. Now, as Chris and I were navigating NICU and seeing our fragile baby fight and recover, fight and recover, fight and recover (the NICU cycle), it was still important to be strong, but it was also essential to learn how to survive the rollercoaster of emotions because my thoughts and feelings would fluctuate a million times within an hour. This did not happen nearly as rapidly during pregnancy, and it was hard to handle during this new phase of NICU.

I was also learning that NICU is a paradoxically quiet yet bustling place. The cast of characters in NICU is large— doctors, nurses, respiratory therapists, PAs, NPs—and they are all on rotation. So, we were dealing with a lot of different people and personalities on a daily basis. Sometimes we clicked, sometimes we didn't, and that was okay.

In a regular birth, the parents can control their environment to be as quiet or bustling as they want. But in NICU, it's out of the parents' control. NICU parents are bombarded by herds of absolutely necessary medical professionals, with their own timelines for intervention and care, and it's hard to find those private, tender moments for bonding. And yet, it is also a calm space where babies are given quietude so they can heal and grow.

That is why there are stringent visitor policies in most NICUs; most family and friends want to chat and coo around the new baby and pass the baby around. That is strictly verboten in NICU. In fact, in acute situations, the parents can't even hold their babies for extended periods of time, never mind pass the baby around to loud relatives.

I also didn't realize until I became a NICU mom that NICU is a place where parents get a crash course in biology and pre-med. Chris and I are liberal arts people; economics for him, history for me. I took one prerequisite, easy-breezy biology class and was lucky to get a C. I never imagined that I would be learning about complex medical issues and, more importantly, that it mattered if I retained the information. This wasn't a test; it was my son's life. I kept a notebook so that I could stay up to speed with all of Tim's medicines, procedures, and next steps.

Part of this process involved being present at "rounds" in NICU. "Rounds," which typically happen in the morning, was a daily meeting in which all the doctors and nurses huddle together to discuss the baby's current condition, his medicine regime, and his next steps. I listened in and took copious notes and rarely missed a round about Tim.

NICU was all these things and more—exhaustion, hormones, recovery from my own surgery, underlying stress, financial concerns about medical bills. The whole experience was daunting, full of sensory and emotion overload. I wanted snuggles, cute onesies, and a serene maternity leave in which I just worried about Tim's sleep schedule and my weight loss plan to get rid of the pregnancy pounds. In short, this was *not* how I pictured my entrée to motherhood.

I discovered that it was difficult for many people, especially other new moms, to relate to what my life was like. I was wise enough, at this point, not to actively engage with optimism bullies, over-empathizers, and platitude people. But I didn't realize that it would be hard to interact with "normal moms."

As I felt robbed of the pregnancy journey, I felt that my new role as mom was stolen from me. I was in a weird purgatory. I was a mom, yet one who would likely go back to work just weeks after delivering Tim so I could save my maternity leave. I was a mom, yet had to rely on a fleet of medical professionals to care for my baby. I was a mom, yet I didn't get to snuggle on demand, or breastfeed, or rely on my own intuition for Tim's needs. Everything was controlled by everyone except me, his mom.

Normal moms can't fathom how challenging NICU can be: how babies teeter on the edge of life and death, how it tests your marriage, how it puts pressure on your non-nuclear family, how it tests your faith, how hard it is to get up to speed with medical information on the fly, how time, days, seasons have no meaning because you spend every waking minute at the hospital, how you couldn't care less about decorating a nursery or developing your weight loss plan, and how medical milestones can be rather graphic.

Most of this perspective came well after my time in NICU especially after having my second, healthy baby. It felt so easy after all I went through with Tim! But I recall that when a friend made the dismissing comment about my son's scar after closure surgery, I put on a happy, brave face and only reported on the good stuff from that moment onwards. I kept the obstacles to myself and Chris or with only the closest family and friends who were full of empathy and had strong stomachs. It wasn't until much later, in some cases years later, that some friends learned that Tim's first few weeks of life were way more serious than a baby having a cold or some other minor setback. I felt like an outsider and had difficulty relating to *normal* moms.

I had anger and sadness during pregnancy, but somehow evaded jealousy. Now, jealousy invaded my life. Jealousy is a mean, green monster (and not the wall at Fenway Park!) and way worse than anger. I'm glad that I actively sought therapy during my time in and after NICU, so I came to a better place with my jealousy and bitterness, but I wish I had more of a prayer mentor during that time because while therapeutic interventions are wonderful, it would have helped to draw strength from the great stories of Biblical heroes. Or to read the Psalms and Proverbs. Or to sit in meditation with God and Mary. That's what I do now. But at the time, this is how I coped, and therapy did help. Over time, I softened and realized that it's not normal moms' fault that they don't get it;

my experience was so traumatic and extreme and unique that only a few get it. And those few are those who have walked the path.

A group of tigers is called a *streak*, and that's what I had: a streak of tigresses, NICU moms. Tigers are solitary creatures, but they are not anti-social. NICU moms are warrior moms, like tigers—unrelenting yet nurturing, fierce yet compassionate, savvy yet respectful. It is this dichotomy that makes them so unique; they are moms first and foremost but must be unyielding in their advocacy and support for their baby. And this balancing act is physically and emotionally exhausting. That's why NICU moms need each other. So I leaned on my streak: Molleen, Lindsay F., Lindsay K., Liz, and Amanda.

Chris was always walking side-by-side with me as well during this difficult NICU journey, of course. I wished at the time there were more resources for dads. I believe there are more opportunities and support groups for NICU dads to connect now than when we were in NICU in 2015. Women seems to build communities very quickly for support. And everyone always asks the moms how they are doing, but dads often get overlooked. I wish that, during our NICU phase, I had been better at asking Chris how he was doing and feeling. No one ever asked him, nor did he have a community of dads with whom to talk.

My fellow NICU moms helped guide me on my new, weird path to motherhood. Molleen was one of my closest friends since childhood—second grade, to be exact. Her family moved to Massachusetts from the Chicago area, and we instantly became friends. Ever since she was a little girl, Molleen was a quirky, smart, and compassionate person. She left Massachusetts by middle school, and even though there was no social media or texting to keep us connected, we sent letters, took airplane rides, and even made VHS videos to stay in touch. Once Facebook became a thing and our modes of communication evolved, it was so much easier to stay in touch because we still lived far apart: she lived in the Bay Area. When she learned of Tim's omphalocele, she was the first friend to ask me how I was doing and demanded a real reply, not some inauthentic happy dance.

Like me, Molleen got pregnant later in life. And once she became pregnant and her daughter was born, she was rushed to NICU because she swallowed meconium. Molleen and her husband, Marc, were in NICU for a week and it was a traumatic experience for their little family. So, Molleen understood; of course, the conditions and the duration were different from our experience, but NICU is NICU: it's scary no matter how long or short you are there.

Molleen sent me care packages, set up a group of her fellow NICU mom friends in which they emailed me every day with simple messages of ways to self-care during NICU, and she checked in with me nearly every day. "How are you do-ing? Thinking of you." These messages were gold to me. She was never an optimism bully, over-empathizer, or platitude person. She would let me vent. She listened. She would say that it sucked because it did. I clung to her emails and texts during my first weeks of NICU. She gave me permission to be honest with myself and my emotions.

I also made new NICU mom friends while I was a mom in the hospital. Enter Lindsay F. The hospital's parent coor-dinator, Courtney, started a program to connect families in which babies were diagnosed with the same condition. There we met Lindsay and her husband and their omphalocele baby a few months before Tim was born. Lindsay and I texted, called, and visited one another often. Cameron is six months older than Tim, so she was busy with a newborn when Tim arrived, and we were new friends so I didn't expect her to have time to spend with me because she still had her own medically fragile baby. But she did. She would call and ask me to coffee. We got our hair blown out together. We did normal mom-friend activities, but our conversations had a much deeper and authentic tone. I am forever grateful that Courtney connected me with Lindsay.

There was another Lindsay in my life—Lindsay K. I met her at the Baby 101 class. We had to give brief introductions, and I mentioned that we were naming our son Timothy. She approached me after the class because she wanted to tell me

how much she loved our name selection. We instantly connected, and I remember confiding in her how scared I was
that I was having a baby with such a significant condition.
But we fell out of touch after the Baby 101 class.

A year later, I ran into Lindsay. She told me that she had
HELLP Syndrome and that her son was born prematurely
and had time in NICU. Our NICU time must have over-
lapped, but we never saw one another on the floor. It was
a terrifying experience for their small family, and they felt
grateful that everyone was healthy after the trauma they endured. Lindsay and I had an instant connection before all this
happened, but now, after our challenging entry into motherhood, our bond was strong. Lindsay and I became playdate
buddies and girls night companions in our post-NICU lives.

And then there was Liz, the dynamo. As I said, NICU
rooms are terrifying, no matter how many tours you have
done of the NICU floor. The persistent beeps and whirs and
hums of the machines never stop. And parents learn what
all the stats mean and panic anytime a number dips below
the threshold number. Liz had a baby who had significant
NICU time, and she was shocked at how antiseptic and scary
the NICU rooms are. Also, she noticed that many families
didn't have any personal affects for their rooms because they
lived so far away from the hospital. Liz, being who she is,
somehow found the time—between having a newborn and
two other children, a demanding job, *and* recovering from

her own NICU trauma—to make care baskets for *all* NICU families at WRPH.

When Chris and I walked into our NICU room, we saw a huge basket full of stuffed animals, books, a blanket, picture frame, and journal. I remember how overcome I was with this basket, thinking, *Who the heck sent this?* When I learned it was from "strangers," I was humbled to my core. I met Liz, weeks later, in the elevator as she was dropping off more baskets. I literally bear-hugged her, in tears, thanking her over and over again.

In NICU, I was keeping my blinders on. As I entered the hospital, I would grab coffee and beeline for our room, not looking into the others' rooms because they were sacred places of bonding and intimacy. But every once in a while, I would sneak a peek, and I would see babies that fit into the palm of a nurse's hand. Or I would see a child who was all covered up and there were special notes on the door to keep very quiet. I was so focused on my own baby—as I should be—that I didn't realize at first that there were forty other moms on the floor quietly struggling just as much as I was.

On the outside, I didn't look like I was struggling. I showered and got dressed in my nice work clothes. And I got my hair blown out each week. My mom gave me a gift card to my salon and somehow had the wisdom and foresight to say, "Katie, you need to feel good about yourself. Go to the salon and get pampered because your next few months will be rough." I did. And they were. (I'm sad to say that weekly hair blow-outs are definitely a thing of the past now.)

There was a tiny, private common area at the entrance to our NICU floor. One morning I was drinking coffee, quietly, by myself. A beautiful, older woman came in and began serving herself coffee. It was her perfume that caught my attention. I let myself relish the beautiful, normal smell. It's not just the OR that is fragrance-free and antiseptic, it feels like the entire hospital environment is sterile as well. That smell! I was in heaven.

In NICU, unlike my regular life, I never interacted with strangers because I was afraid to know what they were going through. And I didn't want to trigger any emotions or compare my story with theirs. So, I avoided all interaction. But now I couldn't help myself. She reminded me of my own mother, who was back in Massachusetts and who I missed so much. "I'm so sorry to bug you, but I love your perfume. The smell makes me feel so normal." Somehow, I didn't cry or reach over and embrace this woman, even though I wanted to. I could feel her warmth and kindness from across the room.

The woman responded in a drawl that can only be explained as honey, "Oh, sweetie. Thank you. I've been watching you on the floor the past few days. And you are a role model for handling this situation. I need to introduce you to my daughter-in-law. She's having trouble with all of this."

I was flattered by the compliment, but I didn't want to be a "role model" for this. I may have looked together on the outside, but on the inside, I still had so many difficult characteristics and emotions: bitterness, jealousy, anger, confusion. Most days, I felt like a little girl who was struggling to make it out of bed and be in NICU with my son. I learned that this woman's daughter-in-law had been blindsided by NICU, whereas I had learned at the twenty-week sonogram.

In many ways, I think being blindsided by NICU is worse than being prepared for it. I can't imagine going through your entire pregnancy, thinking that everything would be perfect, and then a swarm of medical professionals descend upon you and suddenly there are lots of beeps and chaos during the birth process. The confusion and the terror that the parents must feel—I simply can't imagine it. "What's happening? Where's my baby? What is going on?!" I'm making all these thoughts up because I never experienced them and my imagination probably can't capture it at all. But the bottom line is that when a baby needs to be transported for intensive care immediately, the new mom is left behind, wondering, crying, terrified by the turn of events.

There are also many moms who feel the pains of labor before thirty weeks, and their baby is delivered, well before the due date, the size of an iPhone, weighing less than two or three pounds.

I can't even begin to imagine how that must feel, and it's good to be reminded that there are situations out there even more challenging than ours was. Even though my birth experience wasn't what I had hoped and dreamed for, it followed the plan that was created for us. There was minimal trauma during the birth process (the trauma happened during the pregnancy), and more or less, we knew what was in store for us. I like to avoid playing "oppression Olympics"—*Who has it worse, the mom who knew about NICU or the mom who didn't?* because both situations suck. But I lean toward thinking that being blindsided by NICU is worse.

And this family, who I was about to meet, had been blindsided.

I replied to the woman, "Oh gosh, no. I just look like I'm keeping it together, on the outside. This is really hard, and I'm barely keeping above water. I would love to meet your daughter-in-law, if she's up for it. My name is Katie."

"And my name is Ann. My daughter-in-law is Amanda. I will put you both in touch."

She did, and Amanda, my same age, became my rock through NICU.

Amanda is the ying to my yang. I am the oldest of three kids; she is the youngest of five. I can be driven, uptight, and intense; she is relaxed and laid-back. I worked in corporate America; she is an artist. I'm from the Northeast; she's from the Midwest. It seems like we are so opposite that there would be no way that we could navigate this together. But she was the *perfect* person with whom to go through the everyday ups and downs and hardships of having a sick baby. We balanced and complemented one another. I would help her write a list of key questions to ask the surgeons, and she would calm and soothe me when my anxiety reached new heights. We could confide in each other without being overly sentimental. We needed each other, so thank heavens we found each other.

Amanda's newborn son, James, was rushed to NICU unexpectedly because he wasn't breathing correctly after his birth. He had an issue in which his esophagus wasn't connected properly. Amanda was left at the hospital while James (and her husband, Jamie) was rushed to Western Regional Pediatric Hospital. As much as I try to empathize, I cannot imagine what she went through in those moments. (Many years later, a childhood friend told me that her father, who was my English teacher, had the same condition and was the first survivor of this condition. Funny how life is!)

We didn't know it at the time, and even though our sons' conditions were different, we would have almost the identical NICU experience and subsequent hospital visits due to complications. Even if we didn't want to be friends, there was no way we could have avoided our destinies with one another. One of my favorite moments, months after meeting, was when we both wound up on the pediatric floor after yet another medical complication for our little boys.

We weren't even surprised to see each other, rather we were comforted that someone else was going through all this crap too. "Amanda, I have a bottle of wine in my room," I said. "I have Solo cups. Let's meet up in the common room and get wasted."

"Great. I'll be there in five," she replied.

Of course we didn't actually get wasted. We were NICU moms who weren't able to check out in that way—there was too much to do—but it was nice to make a joke. To laugh instead of cry. Amanda was my NICU mom soulmate.

I had been jealous, bitter, and annoyed with people who didn't get it, but there were people who *did* get it. This fellowship of NICU moms, the doctors, the nurses, the therapists, and the hospital chaplain understood what I was going through, so this was my new community. It was within the first four weeks of NICU that I realized: *NICU, while not the path we would ever choose, might not be so terrible. The blessings in this place might outweigh the challenges.* It was my little sliver of hope. For one thing, I wasn't as alone and isolated as I had been during pregnancy. There were always people in NICU, and they were compassionate people. I felt God's compassion through the everyday people in NICU. For this, I thank God for my trials and for the selfless people who carried me through this adversity. When I mourned, I was comforted. God uses ordinary people to do extraordinary things according to His will.

For me, NICU was a place of healing—physically and spiritually. Not only was our medical team healing Tim physically, but they also healed me spiritually.

My metamorphosis from the focused, driven, over-planning careerwoman of September 2014 to the softer, more compassionate person and mom of January 2015 was in full bloom. I felt that I had been generally kind and caring, but now I was developing into someone with more tenderness and grace. My heart was indeed softening.

CHAPTER 11
Viking Baby

It was the middle of February, nineteen days into NICU for our little family. Tim was recovering well from two surgeries, extubation, and withdrawal from big-time narcotics; morphine, fentanyl, and paralytic drugs. I remember asking a doctor, "Is it okay to give this tiny human so many heavy-duty narcotics? Will it affect him, long-term?"

And the doctor replied, "The benefit of these drugs far outweighs the risks. And to be honest, there is no choice. We have to administer these medications, or he won't live. He would go into cardiac or respiratory distress from all the pain." Tim was both a newborn and one of the strongest humans I had ever met.

One time Dr. Cote came in and stated that Tim needed a blood transfusion and that I had to sign consent forms. *Oh my gosh—a blood transfusion? How is this happening to me?* I asked her, "Would you do this if it were your child?"

She responded, "Yes. I wouldn't even think twice about it." So I signed off on it immediately, and Tim received the blood transfusion, which I now call "a power boost" like you see in video games. This was all serious stuff for a novice mom who didn't have any prerequisite medical knowledge.

And Tim. Every mother thinks her child is the most beautiful, the cutest, the absolute best. But my Tim was an amazing wonder-baby. He was the strongest baby I have ever seen. I mean, this kid was and still is fierce, and he lived up to the Bible Scripture that St. Paul instructed to St. Timothy, Tim's namesake, "for God did not give us a spirit of cowardice" (2 Timothy 1:7).

When Tim could finally open his eyes after his closure surgery, he sent me the most intense gaze that I have ever seen. I talked about his Tom Brady tummy. He also had the steely gaze Tom Brady had when he was on a winning drive. The look told me, *Hey, Mom—I got this.* Even as a newborn, he had a fight and intensity that inspired me. I know it's annoying when parents think their newborns have distinct personalities, but Tim really was a strong baby. I saw it. He developed some of his core qualities right from birth because he didn't have a choice: he had to fight to save his own life. I asked the doctors about this intense gaze, and even they echoed it: "The kid is tough. Good luck when he's a teenager!"

I loved comments like that because it meant that we would have a future and a life outside of NICU someday. Years later, I was at a lacrosse game and talking with my friend, Sarah, who is a NICU nurse, and I told her that Tim had an omphalocele and about his strong recovery. She remarked, "You can't be serious. He had closure surgery only a *week* after the silo was placed? Katie, do you get how strong Tim was? And to be able to wean off all those pain meds so well? That's remarkable."

This is how he got his nickname—the Viking Baby—from the medical staff. He was big compared to other babies on the floor, fair-haired, strong, and recovering much quicker than other babies with his condition. A friend sent him a knitted Viking helmet hat, and he wore it for all subsequent surgeries.

While Tim was doing well during his recovery process, our marriage was taking a hit. Though it was only nineteen days to the outside world, our life in NICU had already taken a toll on our relationship. We endured the difficult pregnancy, but NICU felt harder. The addition of a new, healthy baby is a tough adjustment for any couple, no matter how strong their relationship and how prepared they are. There's sleep deprivation, new divisions of labor within the household, decisions about careers, and a new financial column in the budget labeled *BABY*. Now, imagine this stuff with a baby who is critically ill; everything is magnified by at least one hundred percent.

Having a sick baby unearths deep stuff, lurking under the surface that one would hardly want to deal with on a regular day during a courtship, never mind postpartum. We wrestled with questions like: *How do you deal with someone you love who is teetering between life and death? How do you balance work and caring for someone with poor health? What are your coping strategies? Do you have past trauma that may be triggered by NICU?* Hopefully both partners are aligned in their reactions to stress, or they can at least *accept* how their partner processes grief and handles pressure. But if partners aren't aligned, relationships crumble under the pressure.

During NICU, Chris and I, for 80 percent of the experience, were aligned with our roles at the hospital, our processing techniques, our reliance on faith, and how we dealt with stress. But we had our differences about 20 percent of the time with our coping mechanisms—and that 20 percent was more intense than casual disagreements.

For example, Chris found eating out at high-end restaurants to be a source of relief from the NICU experience. But I hated it. I felt guilt for such indulgences: spending all that time and money while our baby was sick in an isolette being watched by strangers. For me, an outlet of comfort was to share our situation, many times to complete strangers, to process and understand what we were going through. Chris would often excuse himself from my impromptu conversations because he could not stand that I was sharing such intimate details about our life.

We fought about these sorts of things.

I remember one fight that got particularly ugly. I was upset, stressed, and frustrated by the entire situation. The helplessness consumed me. I couldn't find anything to calm myself down. Chris said, "Why don't you call your mom? She always seems to put you in a good mood." He was right. I went upstairs to make the phone call. I talked to my mom, and she eased my worries and lifted my spirits.

I bustled down the stairs to tell Chris about my light-hearted conversation with my mom. But during that phone call, it was as if the dark cloud that was hanging over me just moved over to him. He was in a rotten mood and started snapping at me. I can't remember what was said, but it quickly escalated to a shouting match. I was so angry because neither one of us was listening to the other and we were taking low blows at one another. A mug of cold, stale coffee was sitting on an end table. I picked up the coffee cup and threw it against a blank wall with all my force. The coffee mug shattered, and the cold coffee steaked down the wall. I left our condo without cleaning up or apologizing.

During my walk, I thought, "This is bad. We have to get this under control because we can't fight like this. If our home life is like this, we won't make it."

Our hospital had a policy that couples meet with a therapist to discuss how they were feeling during the NICU process. The therapist's name was Jen. I met Jen while I was in the NICU room, but I didn't make an appointment with her. After the fight, I knew that I had to schedule a couple session. I remember the first thing I asked her: "Are we going to make it as a couple?"

After talking through some of our issues and our differing coping mechanisms, she reassured us that we were, in fact, doing well and thought we had a good chance of maintaining, even strengthening, our marriage through this experience. One bad fight and a few differing coping mechanisms wouldn't destroy our relationship. This helped us gain perspective on the big picture.

But I still wasn't convinced. "But we haven't even been married for a year, and we had a whirlwind romance. If we had been married longer, would this be easier?" I asked.

"Not necessarily," she replied. "It doesn't matter how long or short you've been together or married. Nothing will prepare you for a critically sick, fragile child. Not even coping with a dying parent. When a parent dies, which is sad and heart-breaking, it is the natural order of things. Watching your child struggle and suffer while you are well is not natural for any couple. It causes tension and with tension comes conflict. But there are ways you can handle the conflict better."

And over the course of our NICU experience, Jen helped us do just that. She encouraged us to do date nights; she even had Dr. Cote write us a prescription for it. She also told us to try to get some normalcy in our lives: maintaining our routines, going home every night from NICU at a reasonable time, and partaking in social events with our friends.

And there was a major social event, considered an unofficial holiday by many Americans, the upcoming weekend—the Super Bowl. That year, 2015, the New England Patriots made it to the Super Bowl, much to the chagrin of the locals rooting for the Broncos. Chris and I were going to a party hosted by our friend Dan, who was also a die-hard Patriots fan. This would be our first social outing since Christmas. And our Christmas was *very* quiet.

Chris decided to visit the NICU only briefly the morning of the Super Bowl because he was exhausted from his work-NICU-home routine. He needed a few hours to rest and recover by himself. Because of couples counseling, I was better at listening to him and understood his need for solitude. We were working hard to communicate and express our needs. So, I went to NICU after Chris left so that Tim had a steady stream of visitors (Chris and me!). We agreed to meet at the party.

On the big day, I brought Tim a little Patriots shirt that a friend gave me, and I had on my Tom Brady jersey. I brought an extra Gronkowski jersey to the hospital that I was planning to drape over Tim's isolette.

When I arrived in NICU, I asked Tim's nurse, Katie, for help putting Tim's little Patriots T-shirt on. I still wasn't 100% comfortable moving or changing him by myself. She remarked, "This is so awesome! I'm so glad I am assigned to you guys because I'm also a Pats fan. I grew up in Massachusetts."

Oh, yes! We got the perfect nurse for the day. I offered her the Gronk shirt, and she promptly put it over her scrubs.

It got better. "Where in Massachusetts are you from? I grew up north of Boston in North Andover."

She replied, "I grew up in Foxboro."

I couldn't contain myself. *Are you kidding me? Our assigned nurse for today couldn't be any more perfect. Her name is Katie, like me. She grew up in Foxboro, home of Gillette Stadium, where the Patriots play, and she is our nurse for today all the way out West?!*

I replied, "I just can't. This is too much. Foxboro? Are you *serious*? Did you go to school in Massachusetts too?"

Nurse Katie responded, "Yeah, I started at Holy Cross—"

I think I may have roared, "STOP. IT! I graduated from Holy Cross too! STOP!"

"—but I transferred to James Madison after my freshman year," she finished.

That's okay. No one is perfect. But my goodness, how did all these coincidences happen? It was bigger than me. I knew, right then and there, that the Pats would win that day.

The craziness of NICU had made me forget about my prayer life and God and Mary. But they were still there, in these tiny moments, telling me that everything would be okay. Again, God not only dwells with us and in us, but sometimes we don't realize it, so God also actively seeks us. I wasn't intentionally turning away, but I'd been thinking, *Thanks, God, I got it now. I can do it "my" way. I got it from here.* But God was gently bringing me back to Him. God seeks us in the wilderness of our lives. And these coincidences were just His way of telling me He was there. And He's always there.

I wanted to stay with Tim and Nurse Katie to watch the game, but there weren't TVs in NICU. And I had made the original plan to meet up with Chris at Dan's Super Bowl party anyway. I was sad to leave Tim, but I was looking forward to the party. It had been a long time since I had interacted with friends in a jovial setting.

It turns out that I should have prepared myself better for my first real social engagement in months. The anxiety I suffered from during this party was overwhelming.

As I learned during the pregnancy, life still carries on even when there is trauma. I got this message again, loud and clear, on Super Bowl Forty-Nine, when the Patriots faced the Seahawks. I walked into the hopping party and felt like I'd been knocked over by a huge ocean wave. I was unused to large crowds and loud noise because my world was so quiet, small, and controlled in the NICU. Terrified, I searched for Chris like a separated child scrambles for her parent. *Where is he?*

I found him at the back of the house and nearly clung to him. I didn't tell him how I was feeling. I thought I would get a beer and find a seat. My impromptu plan was to just watch the game and not talk. But I knew a lot of people at the party!

"Katie! How are you doing? Where's the kid?"

"Katie! You look great. Where's your baby? Go Pats!"

"Katie, you Masshole—how ya doing, kid?"

I felt bombarded by normal party banter. My natural ease and humor were unavailable. I ran to the bathroom in a panic. *How am I going to survive this party? What do I say? How do I tell people that my baby is in NICU? Do people even know what NICU is? And how do I say it—light-heartedly or should I give them the blow-by-blow?* I was in unfamiliar territory, and I was scrambling to create a plan.

When I was pregnant, I'd created pitches to explain my situation to different audiences. But I hadn't been around friends since Tim was born, so I didn't have anything planned. After this party, I created one: "Tim has a condition in which his organs grew outside of his body. He's already had two surgeries, and he is recovering at the hospital. It's been tough, but Tim is a little fighter and we have a great support system and medical team. Please pray for us, though. Prayers work."

But I hadn't thought of that sensible soundbite yet. Instead, I was drowning in a huge crowd that should have been a ton of fun. I bumbled through the party, oversharing medical details to one mom until her eyes glazed over, light-heartedly telling another guy that I could easily complete medical school after the past three weeks, giving the detailed explanation of an omphalocele to an interested listener. I didn't talk about the Patriots. I didn't ask anyone questions about themselves. I was focused on myself because I had lost sight of anything other than Tim's condition. As someone who works in sales, I *know* to ask questions about others in order to spark conversation. But instead, I was a colossal fail.

I had failed at having fun. As I surrendered to the feeling of disappointment and sadness, a kind woman, Julie, who I only knew a bit, invited me to sit next to her. She was a social worker, and I think she had picked up on my confused, defeated vibe. She didn't talk to me much or ask questions about Tim; she just hung out with me, and we watched the game together. Her calm, gentle aura relaxed the tension building in my body. She will never know it, but I was so grateful for her gentle spirit that day. She carried me through the party. And that's the wonder of going through a tough time: strangers can be everyday heroes. We see it throughout the Bible and in the stories of Jesus, but it's hard to think it can happen in your own life.

It turned out that my prediction—based on all the co-incidences that morning with Foxboro-Holy-Cross Nurse Katie—was correct. The Patriots won in dramatic fashion with a Patriots interception on Seattle's one-yard line to clinch the game. Though the Patriots' win wasn't a particular victory for Tim, it felt symbolic to me that life was moving in the right direction.

The day after the Super Bowl, on NICU day twenty-three, Tim was abruptly transferred to the step-down NICU. He no longer needed the urgent and acute care of Level 4 team. Now, he could focus on his feeding and growing.

The transfer was set to happen right at shift change, before the night nurses took over. Nurse Jill, Tim's primary nurse in Level 4, stayed a little extra to participate in this momentous moment with us. I called Chris at work, "Chris! Come quickly. Tim is graduating to the step-down NICU!" It is a big NICU moment, and I knew he wouldn't want to miss it. Sure enough, Chris was able to drop everything and leave work to be there for me and Tim.

The transition to the step-down NICU is a joyful, mile-stone moment, often referred to as "graduation day" for our mighty littles, but once we were settled in there, I immediately struggled with the transition. In Level 4 there is an urgency to everyday life. In the step-down NICU, it is much calmer. Tim's recovery was moving in the right direction—much faster than anyone anticipated—yet my body and mind were still in fight-or-flight mode. I couldn't seem to get my nervous system to calm down for step-down NICU. I joked that it was because I was a Northeasterner who couldn't chill out in the tranquil vibe of life in the West, but I knew it was deeper than a silly stereotype.

I was also oddly scared by Tim's progress. *Would our progress be like a kid who peaks early in a sport and then fizzles out?* It seemed like a lousy comparison, but it was all I could think of. Much like during the pregnancy journey, I was waiting for the other shoe to drop in NICU. I didn't allow myself the elation that I should have felt and instead reminded myself that Tim may be in step-down NICU for the next five to eight months as Dr. Cote had forecasted. As a former marathon runner, I knew I had to pace myself and approach Tim's recovery much like a marathon: slow and steady.

There was another transition during this time: I went back to work. As Dr. Cote had told me, "Katie, go back to work and save your maternity leave. Please, trust me when I say that this is the best, and most expensive, day care you will ever have. Take advantage of it while you can." It wasn't the advice I wanted to hear, but I knew she was right. There would be a day that Tim would be discharged, and it would be gut-wrenching to leave him home with a nanny because my maternity leave had been used up while he was in NICU.

I communicated this back-to-work plan to my manager, Mike, and he agreed. I filed all the paperwork with HR. I went back to work twenty-nine days after Tim's birth, a week after he was transitioned to the step-down NICU. My brain knew this was the best possible decision given the circumstances. But my body, nervous system, and heart felt differently. It wasn't what I wanted, but at this point, I felt that I was powerless to achieve anything I desired.

The Super Bowl Party was a blessing because it was a little preview of the draining feeling of going back to work. The first few days took my breath away. All this change, all this transition, all this trauma in such a short period of time. Within my twenty-nine days away, I had given birth, prepared my newborn for two life-threatening surgeries, left the hospital without my baby, made huge decisions about blood transfusions and narcotics withdrawals, moved from Level 4 NICU to step-down NICU, and now, I had to go back to work and function like none of this had happened.

When I was a kid, my family rented a beach house in Rhode Island on a rocky beach with big waves. One day, I was playing in the ocean, farther out than my siblings and cousins, and the undertow swept me up in a terrifyingly strong current. I was drawn into the ocean, knowing I was in danger and powerless. Just as I surrendered, the ocean showed mercy and heaved me back to shore in a messy summersault, inhaling the briny seawater like I was slurping an enormous oyster, scraping up my back on the rocky shore. I came out of the ocean, dazed, bloodied, and terrified, but I didn't say anything because I didn't want anyone to think I was a wimp who couldn't handle a few big waves. That's how I felt on NICU day twenty-nine when I went back to work.

I wish I had the spiritual perspective that I've since learned: "For whenever I am weak, then I am strong" (2 Corinthians 12:10). It seems paradoxical. How can I be weak and strong at the same time? In our weakness, our vulnerability, our difficult time, we are growing stronger. And for me, much later on, I realized that this feeling of simultaneous weakness and strength was a reminder of the cross. Jesus in His profound suffering on the torturous cross emptied Himself and died so we live. Jesus conquered death, sin, and the cross, and that is strength—even though His human form was so physically weak. Here I was with my own cross: my exhausting life as a new mom to a sick baby. And while my cross felt heavy and I felt weak, I wish I realized how strong I was becoming. There is power and strength in weakness.

The routine of work did help calm me down. As during my pregnancy, my management team showed compassion and flexibility for my situation, and I settled into my old normalcy within a week. At first, I liked the routine, but I soon realized that I had changed. I didn't care about work the same way I did before. But at that point, I was too emotional to discern my true feelings, and it didn't make sense to make a major decision—like quitting my job—when I was under duress. So, I continued on. I had to do what I had to do.

Unlike my job in New York City where I traveled and often worked from home, in this role I was chained to my desk. They had strict guidelines about being in the office, and it frustrated me to have so much importance placed on having your butt in the chair when I was such an experienced professional. But Mike, Kyle, and John (the latter two were Mike's bosses) knew that I was a key asset to the team and would let me work on Mars if need be. So I spent a lot of time in the hospital's conference rooms reserved for working parents.

Many can't believe that I went back to work when my baby was only five weeks old. Looking back on it, I can't believe it either. I was still recovering from the C-section, but I was running on adrenaline and commitment to my new, little family. I would do anything to save time for when Tim came home so I could have the serene maternity leave of which I had always dreamed.

So, life went on this way for many weeks. I thought it would be this way indefinitely because of our estimated six-to-nine-month NICU stay, so I prepared myself for the grind. I was in a weird purgatory of office life and motherhood in the NICU. It was not the best place to be, but I had to accept it.

On NICU day thirty-one, and a few days after being back at work, Chris and I walked into Tim's room and saw a gaggle of doctors and nurses hovering over his crib. *Oh! They are just looking at how cute and overly responsive he is,* my proud, new-mama heart thought. Then my heart sank. I remembered my fellow NICU moms telling me, "If a lot of doctors and nurses are huddled in your room, something is wrong." Before anyone said anything, I changed my thought process—something was wrong with Tim.

"Hi, Katie, Chris. Tim has a hernia. We will have to repair it in the next couple of days," said Dr. Harris, the neonatologist on rotation that day, skipping any pleasantries. I didn't mind—I wanted him to cut to the chase.

I was crest-fallen. Up until this point, Tim had breezed through his recovery process, given the condition he had. So much that his estimated NICU time was cut in half, which I chose not to believe so that I wouldn't be disappointed if it turned out to be the original Fourth of July forecast. This was his first hiccup in the NICU journey, and it hit me and Chris hard. I started to cry.

"Oh no. This isn't a big surgery. This is an easy one," said Dr. Harris.

After all that I know now, he was right. Hernia repairs are easy-breezy surgeries, even for tiny humans. But at the time, I was a newbie to this NICU thing.

"No surgery is easy," I tearfully responded.

"You are right. No surgery is easy. But please trust me that this recovery is quick. And we don't have a choice. We have to repair."

Dr. Harris was right: a hernia repair was easy, and the recovery was swift.

But I had only been two days back to work and my kid had to have surgery, his third in his five-week-old life. *Will this drama ever stop?* I asked myself. *When will my life feel boring and easy and fun again? Or will it always be like this? Like I'm being chased by a giant bear and never get any rest?*

CHAPTER 12

Bottle-Feeding Our Way Home

As someone who looks at food and gains weight, I could not imagine how gaining weight could be an issue. But as I was soon to learn, it is very difficult for some babies and adults.

Tim did not develop the sucking reflex that most babies naturally have. Because he was intubated and received food (TPN) through a central line for the first seventeen days of his life, he didn't know how to suck and take in food orally. We tried breastfeeding right after he was extubated but, as I recounted, that didn't work out so well. Now, Chris and I had to learn how to bottle-feed Tim. This would prove to be our biggest obstacle in our NICU journey, so much so that feeding issues prevented us from going home. The idea that feeding was Tim's primary problem felt like some sort of crazy joke, the biggest irony in the world: I have spent a lifetime of dieting to *avoid* gaining weight, and now I have a kid who can't gain weight?

I didn't care that I couldn't breastfeed him, but there is a sadness and helplessness in watching your child refuse food. It's a primal instinct to feed your baby, however you do it. When Tim wouldn't eat, they placed an NG tube (feeding tube) through his nose that led to his tummy. In this way, he was fed every two hours. In Level 4 NICU, I intellectually knew that modern medicine saved my baby. But it wasn't until this phase of feeding that I really saw that science was keeping my baby alive. The medical world has evolved to a point of creating man-made food with proper nutrition that could be administered this way through an NG tube, nourishing my sick baby when natural methods weren't working. *Yay, science! Sorry I hated you in high school.*

We started with the NG tube, exclusively. They called it *gavage*, which sounded so French. "Oh, yes, Tim, it's time for you to be gavaaaaaged." I loved saying it, but I didn't love that he relied on it. And I was worried he would go home with his NG tube. At this point, he was an active baby and often ripped it out of his nose. How could I possibly put that thing back through his nose and accurately guide it down his throat to his stomach? I couldn't. I knew I would miss the right angle, and he would aspirate the formula. I was scared.

While I didn't want Tim to come home on an NG tube, I did want him to have a G-tube, which is inserted through the abdomen, directly to the stomach. Tim was so small he wasn't even on the growth chart for his age. No one was particularly stressed about this. I mean, the kid had been through a lot! But my family is big—always at least in the eightieth percentile in weight and height. And when my friends were bragging on Facebook about having these big, ninety-fifth-percentile chubsters, I felt defeated as a mom. I had seen a G-tube first-hand because James, Amanda's son, had a G-tube, and he was growing bigger and stronger by the day. In fact, we were still in this feeding abyss when they got discharged. I was happy for Amanda, but I wondered when it was our turn to go home. I begged the nurses and doctors, "Can we please get Tim a G-tube? I want him to get big. And I want to go home."

"Katie, we can't. Tim is not anatomically correct. It would be irresponsible for us to try to insert a G-tube into his stomach when we don't really know where his stomach is."

We had to get this kid to drink a bottle.

But it was torture. Nurse after nurse patiently worked with Tim so he would learn to suck and accept the bottle. We had to try a few different formulas until we found one that he tolerated. I just watched and learned. Days passed, and progress was slow. Our NICU journey went from sprinting in Level 4 to a complete standstill in step-down NICU. The progress was so minuscule that it was hard to get excited about milestones. "Ooh, he drank thirty milliliters at eleven a.m. and then thirty-five milliliters at five p.m.!" He should have been drinking at least sixty milliliters per feeding at that point.

I was so frustrated. And at times, while I was struggling to bottle-feed him, I would turn to the nurse, and say, "Forget it. Just gavage him. This isn't working." I resigned myself to being here until the Fourth of July, still in bottle torture.

Then Nurse Jessica kicked my butt and wouldn't enable my helplessness. She was a fellow marathon runner, boy mom, and overall badass. She pushed me not to give up so easily.

"Oh, Katie, stop it. You are tougher than this," she admonished me. "You *will* feed him. He *will* take the bottle. Here, let's do it together."

I loved Nurse Jessica. She wasn't an optimism bully. She believed in Tim and Chris and me.

Over time, Tim started taking more volume through the bottle. And his gavage French *dejeuners* were becoming less and less. Then I overheard one of the doctors speaking to a nurse about Tim: "I would give him another week, two weeks tops, and the McCarty family is ready to go home."

It was only the fourth week in February. Tim had spent thirty-seven days (six weeks) in NICU, and they were talking about sending him home within the next two weeks. *Am I hearing this correctly?* Chris and I were truly planning to be in NICU until the Fourth of July. Even though the days felt long, and the duration felt much longer than six weeks, this was way shorter than the timeframe we expected.

One would think that we would be ecstatic with the news. Yes, we were relieved. But we also felt unprepared and scared to take Tim home. I joked during the pregnancy that I didn't care about a nursery, but I really *didn't* have a nursery ready. And we didn't have any clothes for him because we knew he would have multiple surgeries and didn't know what clothes he would be able to wear, so we relied on the hospital's donated clothes. I still needed to buy all those bottles and specialized formula. And I never got around to making a "meet the pediatrician" meeting prior to his birth, so Tim didn't even have a pediatrician lined up! My mind went into dizzying overdrive.

Looking back on it, it makes me think of the story of when Jesus "pops in" for a visit with Martha and Mary. Martha is so frantic, preparing the home for his arrival because he is, of course, such a special guest, while Mary is attentively present with Jesus. Martha is exasperated that Mary isn't helping with the tasks of hospitality that she tells Jesus (?!) to nag Mary to help her more. But Jesus gently reminds Martha that she is too occupied with the wrong things. Instead, she should be like her sister, Mary, who is living in the moment. This lesson is so important. Yes, it's good to be prepared, organized, and hospitable, but the most important part is being present to the moment. I had become so focused on my tasks, I was losing sight of what was most important: Tim's homecoming.

Once my mind settled, I realized this was all material, easy stuff. I just needed a few hours at Target to buy all the baby stuff and I could make the appropriate phone calls to order the formula and reschedule that meeting with the pediatrician that we had selected. What was *really* bothering me? I didn't need to dig deep to understand why I held back all my joy of coming home: I was terrified of caring for this fragile baby all by myself. That imaginary, serene maternity leave that I dreamed of was just that, a dream. *How could I handle this fragile baby by myself?*

In the hospital, I had doctors and nurses and specialists and therapists buzzing around me all the time. If I had a question, they were there. If I needed an extra set of hands, they were there. If Tim's demeanor changed suddenly, I had all the resources needed to see if it was a real problem or just regular newborn stuff. When we got home, who would help me?

I confided these fears to Nurse Jessica. She listened intently. And she encouraged me that I knew way more than I was giving myself credit. "Katie, you are a great mom. Please don't doubt yourself. Tim is amazing, and you will handle anything. And if you get scared, just call us here. Katie, really, you've got this." Her words soothed me and gave me the encouragement I needed to make this transition to home.

Nurse Jessica carried me over the finish line of our NICU marathon.

I got the official phone call while I was at work. It was Dr. Kelley, the head neonatologist, and he left a message. I still have the message, saved on my hard drive. "Katie, this is Dr. Kelley. It looks like Timmy is doing great, and he just needs to feed well today. So yeah, he is ready to come home tomorrow or the day after tomorrow. I'm here all day if you want to call me back. Congratulations!"

I was in shock, even though I had been in the trenches every day, actively a part of his healing. I called Chris. "Chris, Tim is going to be discharged tomorrow or the next day! Can you believe it?!"

Chris cheerfully replied, "*Yes!* I can't wait!"

We had to make all the logistical plans for Tim to come home. The first thing I had to do was talk to Mike and tell him that part two of my maternity leave was about to begin—the remaining seven weeks that I saved.

Chris met me at the hospital to start the initial stages of the discharge process. We sat with an administrator to figure out the best day to leave, based on Tim's current status and the availability of personnel to help us leave. We were also offered to do a "practice night" before we went home. The "practice night" was a private room on the NICU floor with a queen-sized bed and a crib to simulate the experience of being at home, together. Tim would be wire- and monitor-free, just like he would be at home. Chris and I would practice with night feedings—something we had never done because we always went home at night. But we did have a safety net; if anything went wrong, we could just call for a doctor or nurse who was right down the hall. This was exactly the baby step we needed before going home where we would be all by ourselves.

The practice night went smoothly, and we were discharged on the second Friday in March. It had been fifty-four days (seven weeks and five days) since Tim was born. We had great joy and gratitude for the amazing medical staff at WRPH. We left the hospital thinking that our days there were over and we could fully jump into the next chapter of our lives; our troubles were behind us. NICU, surgeries, drama—it was all behind us, and we were ready for a peaceful journey into parenthood. I thought we were at the journey's end of this NICU marathon. And yes, it was an end to NICU.

But as I was about to learn, there is no finish line for a medically complex baby like Tim.

PART III

THE NEW NORMAL

CHAPTER 13

Homecoming

Chris, Tim, and I left the hospital without any fanfare. While I was pregnant, I envisioned that we would exit NICU with a festive, loud farewell. But time in NICU reshaped my expectations of what bringing home a baby was like. The intense day-to-day of NICU, even in step-down, had been driving my adrenaline, keeping me physically and intellectually present for Tim. But now, I was experiencing the emotional exhaustion, and that made me want to go home quietly, finally, with no big to-do about it.

When I ran the Philadelphia Marathon back in 2001, I planned a big party after the race. But as I was showering after the run, I thought, *Why am I doing this? I am so exhausted. I just want to blow-dry my hair, get dressed, curl up on my bed, and celebrate next week, if at all.* Just like I had learned then, I now knew I wanted a quiet homecoming. Chris agreed. It felt like my intuition and inner voice were coming back to me.

Little did we know how unprepared we were for what to do with a newborn.

Chris and I lived a short fifteen-minute drive away from the hospital, but we drove so slowly that it took nearly triple the time to get home. I joked to Chris that people would think he was driving high—the area had recently legalized marijuana—and not that he had a fragile newborn aboard.

I wanted Tim to have the perfect, though quiet, homecoming; presenting his room was the highlight. "Tim, look! It's your new room!" I exclaimed when I carried him in. Once we'd heard the whispers that Tim would be coming home much sooner than we thought, we had rushed to Target, bought all the necessities, and clicked *Buy Now* on the items waiting in our Amazon shopping cart. We managed to put together a beautiful nursery in three days, a small miracle in and of itself. As the saying goes, a lot can happen in three days!

"Tim, your room," I said again. We treated the moment as if he were a five-year-old we had just adopted, a child who might be capable of exclaiming, "*I love it!* Thank you, Mommy and Daddy!" Those two months had accelerated and condensed our parenting process so much it felt like five years had already passed. We experienced more highs and lows during pregnancy and NICU than many parents face over the course of many years.

But he just squawked and cooed, as babies do.

"Let's go for a walk!" Chris suggested.

That sounded like a perfect idea. After all, Tim had been cooped up in the hospital just shy of two months. He had never seen the world outside of those walls! We couldn't wait to have this special milestone—a simple walk outside—with our newborn son.

We wanted to do normal things that we couldn't do in NICU. It was a warm day in early March, but we bundled Tim up in a heavy fleece snowsuit-like outfit for a walk in our neighborhood. Chris assembled the stroller, and we cautiously started our walk. Not even ten minutes in, Tim started wailing. Everything, even simple things, felt hard because of the intensity of NICU. Our nervous systems were still wired for a five-alarm fire instead of a routine situation.

"*WAAAH. WAAAH.*"

It was Tim's first meltdown without all the doctors and nurses to help us to console him.

"Chris, Chris, Chris—what do we do? Chris!"

"Katie, I don't know. Um . . . where's some shade?"

There wasn't any shade close by. I said it was warm, but now it felt blazing hot. This was my first moment of soothing my newborn baby on my very own. And while I had the best Mommy Bootcamp, thanks to the NICU nurses, I was unable to calm down Tim. I knew what to do, but I was paralyzed by the sensory overload *and* having too many techniques that I had learned. I hadn't had the one-on-one time with Tim nor the regular practice time to know what worked best for him. I felt defeated.

We scurried back to the safety of our home.

It was such a small moment, so minor really, but it summarized our first day together as a family.

When we got home, we realized that we had put the toddler insert in the baby stroller instead of the infant one. We didn't even know where the infant one was and had to go searching. This detail had a lot of significance: we hadn't prepared to bring a newborn home. Most of our preparation was for a six-to-twelve-month-old baby because we thought Tim would be in the hospital for longer. We had just survived a lot of trauma and were trying to figure out this "new normal," and that meant figuring out life outside of NICU and learning things that ought to be intuitive.

When I read mommy blogs about how new moms were tired and overwhelmed and worried about inane things, I would just shake my head and think, *Spend a day in NICU. Then you will really know what it is to be overwhelmed.*

My self-righteous NICU mom superiority complex was in full force. I wasn't proud of having these thoughts and feelings, but I had to accept them in order to eventually move past them. Without the distraction and drama of the NICU, I had to *feel* my feelings now, and they were a nasty cocktail made by a college student mixing together a half-dozen conflicting spirits. I was overwhelmed yet focused, exhausted but present, quiet but joyful, grateful yet bitter. A deep bitterness that had been lurking beneath the surface the entire time was finally emerging.

Tim's estimated NICU time was cut by more than half. I couldn't have asked for a better NICU medical team and support system. I had a fellowship of wonderful NICU moms with whom I could share my highs and lows. *So why was I so negative? Why this bitterness, jealousy, and air of superiority? And why were these feelings dominating me instead of joy and gratitude?* I can see now, all these years later, that the experience had cut to the core of me: my worthiness as a mother. I think this issue haunted me the whole time, but all the other emotions were easier to diagnose. All the while, I searched for reasons why this happened to me, how I must have done something wrong to deserve all this hardship. And now, it felt like whiplash: I wondered what I did to deserve such a short NICU duration and all the blessings bestowed upon me. I didn't feel worthy of it. And paradoxically, I felt jealous of other mothers who didn't question their worthiness.

I wish the post-NICU me could tell NICU me that the prenatal diagnosis and the time in NICU weren't her fault, just as much as the speedy recovery and homecoming weren't gifts for virtuous behavior. God doesn't deliver our life events based on a behavior scorecard. He works in ways far more mysterious than our human comprehension. And no matter what the outcome is, God loves us, and He wants us to abide in his love and know we are worthy of His love. Yet, at the time, this underlying, undiagnosed feeling of unworthiness gnawed at me.

This feeling often made it hard to interact with others, even when people wanted to visit us. I had been warned by other NICU moms to keep visitors to a minimum when we got home: NICU babies need rest and quiet to heal and grow. They also have fragile immune systems, and we didn't want to worry about mysterious germs lurking in our home. This medical truth, along with my intense array of feelings, was keeping me incredibly isolated. My attempt to control Tim's environment so he would stay healthy was also driving me crazy. It was like those stories of royals finally having an heir and then doing *everything* to keep the child healthy—completely isolating him from the world to such an extent that he wound up crippled by fear, codependence, and entitlement. The comparison was a little extreme, but I knew I had to snap myself out of this over-controlling paranoia or Tim would end up as a timid, dependent shell of a little boy kept in a bubble.

This is a common problem for NICU parents: how do you protect your fragile baby but allow them to have normalcy with the outside world? This conundrum occurs well after NICU time and extends far into childhood. After a week of being home, Chris and I finally accepted our first visitors. It was a small step but an essential one.

We had also incorporated physical therapy into our routine. When Tim started PT while still in the hospital, I had thought it funny that a newborn would need such a service. Wasn't PT just something you did when you sprained your ankle or tore your ACL? NICU babies often need PT to engage the muscles that were dormant while they endured surgery and, subsequently, rested for recovery. Once a week, Connor, our physical therapist, came to our house to assist Tim in achieving his gross motor developmental milestones, such as rolling over and crawling, in an appropriate time frame.

Despite our unsuccessful first stroll in the park, my fear of visitors, and some difficult emotions, things did finally start to flow better. It started to feel like the "real" maternity leave I had always dreamed of was coming true.

But the ease abruptly ended one day when I noticed that Chris had an awful-looking rash covering his chest and stomach. I asked him if it hurt; it looked so raw and angry. "Did you change detergents?" he asked me. I hadn't. Over the next two days, Chris's rash spread from his stomach and chest to his entire back, and he was in excruciating pain. The doctor confirmed that it was shingles.

I couldn't believe this was happening. We were trying, valiantly, to settle into our new normal, and now poor Chris had a painful dose of shingles. I felt that the stress of the NICU was finally catching up with him and manifesting in a painful, physical ailment. At the same time, my thoughts pivoted to Tim. *Oh my gosh. What about Tim? Shingles* must *be a cousin to chickenpox. And Tim hasn't been vaccinated for chickenpox yet. Oh my goodness, what do we do?*

We called our new pediatrician's office and the NICU and explained the situation. We got the same response from both resources: "There is no data to suggest that shingles can be transferred to a baby and induce something like chickenpox in the baby. There are no reported cases of this scenario. However, to be on the extra-cautious side, quarantine the parent with shingles for a few days."

When Chris left to quarantine at his parents' home, I felt sad and terrified to be all alone with our fragile Tim. If perspective were a fire alarm, mine was out of batteries and chirping incessantly. It no longer let me know *this is a big deal* or *this isn't a big deal.* The alarm was just chirping and chirping; everything felt like a *very big deal.*

I knew I needed a plan. I did not want to be alone while Chris was away, so I created a rotation of "nurses" to help me with Tim. I called my friends, Ashleigh, Kaitlin, Cara, my sister-in-law Jennifer, and my mother-in-law Susan. They all responded affirmatively to my call to duty. Instead of loneliness and tears, I shared gossip, fun, and wine with my girlfriends as they helped me. In some ways, it was an escape. It finally felt like I was getting that elusive mama village that many new moms describe. *Maybe my bitterness will soften faster than I thought,* I hoped. The few days passed quickly, Chris's shingles disappeared, and our little family resumed life together.

Chris settled back in, and we had a few weeks of sleep-deprived, snuggly, and happy days of baby coos, stroller walks, and homemade dinners at our condo. We slowly had visitors trickle in, one by one, to keep the environment stable and healthy for Tim. It was wonderful. We finally got to the place of calm and peace I so desperately hoped for.

One of the blessings of having such a traumatic pregnancy and extended NICU stay was that I never took a newborn moment for granted. Once I stopped panicking when he was upset, I loved every cry, every feeding, every midnight wake-up call, everything about being a new mom. I didn't feel resentful that this little creature was consuming my every moment; I loved it.

The only cloud was that I was about to be at the end of my seven weeks of maternity leave at home. The second week of my maternity leave was a blip when Chris had to leave because of his shingles, but we had stability for the next four weeks.

A unique benefit of having a baby in NICU is that they come home on a schedule. Tim was predictable with his naps and bedtime routine, and I followed the same schedule he had in NICU. I also kept a detailed log for his feedings, his sleep schedule, and even a record of his poop and pee. I felt that if anything went wrong, I had to know *exactly* when something went south. It was particularly important for me to track his feeding because his weight was being carefully monitored by his outpatient medical team.

Then, eight days before the end of my maternity leave, I was jolted, yet again, from my newfound sense of routine when I heard Tim coughing at four a.m. I went into his room and observed a wet, coarse cough that sounded much too big for his little body. His breath was labored. I woke Chris up, and he came into the room to listen. "Oh yeah, Katie. That doesn't sound good. Let's call the pediatrician." I was relieved that he had the same reaction; I was still having difficulty discerning what was a real or a phantom problem.

I called the pediatrician at four thirty, and the on-call nurse picked up. "Hello? Name and birth date of your child." I gave the information. And before she could even ask what the problem was, she heard Tim's cough in the background. "Is that your four-month-old with that cough?" There was no hesitation in her voice.

"Yes. That's why I am calling."

"You need to go into the ER. That cough isn't right."

Panic swept through my body, but I had to keep moving, pack a bag, and collect my baby. I thought the hospital was behind us. I had done a delayed birth announcement so I didn't jinx anything after his NICU experience. And it was an unusual birth announcement; it listed his medical accomplishments with pictures from my iPhone instead of professional photos. When I sent that birth announcement, it was my way of saying, *We are done with the hospital.*

I didn't navigate the grief and sadness during pregnancy and NICU perfectly, but one thing I had done well: except for my initial feelings of entitlement of a healthy pregnancy and perfect Colin, I never let myself create expectations. I relied on the experts. I leaned on my fellow NICU moms. I kept God and Mary on my radar. I let go of outcomes and focused on the process of Tim healing.

But when we went home, something in my brain and heart shifted. I let myself have expectations, finally. I *expected* that he would be stable. I *expected* that Tim would be healthy once he was home, that NICU was a just blip in his beautiful life. I *expected* that I would snap out of my bitterness. But expectations are just premeditated resentments, as they say. And I was seething with resentment. *This isn't fair. It's not fair to me, to Chris, and especially Tim. Tim didn't ask for any of this, yet he's been poked and prodded and deprived of exploring his new world as newborns are supposed to.* The feeling of unfulfilled expectations was so crushing, I went back to my trauma scorecard that I had subconsciously kept during pregnancy.

Haven't I checked off all the boxes of paying my dues at this point? Isn't it time for peace, stability, and happiness? I expected those things after all I had endured. Instead, what did I get? I got a husband with shingles, a truncated maternity leave, and an ER visit.

I wish I had known then what I know now—to pray. But instead, I decided to close the door on prayer, even those prayers of lament. Because somewhere, deep down, in a part of me I couldn't even touch, I thought I was unworthy of motherhood.

My willpower to temper my expectations was gone. I was worn and weary, and my expectations couldn't be battled with anymore. This wasn't a pity party—it was a pity tantrum. I knew, intellectually, that I needed to turn to a higher power, but I was pissed at God, so I turned away from Him.

As we rushed out the door, I felt so afraid and so, so alone.

CHAPTER 14

Pediatric Floor

Dawn was breaking as we pulled up to the hospital, the same one in which Tim had just spent fifty-four days. Even with all our medical drama, I had never been to the ER before. I'd always imagined it to be a hectic, crazy experience where you wait for hours, just like on TV shows. But it was quiet. We calmly walked to the front desk, gave our information, reason for being there, and were admitted right away.

The pediatric ER doctor prodded Tim's little body as he coughed and coughed. They did all the usual processes for admitting a child to the hospital. Then they put a pulse oximeter on his big toe to observe his oxygen levels. That's when the pediatric ER doctor said, "It looks like RSV. His oxygen levels are too low. We need to admit him."

RSV stands for respiratory syncytial virus. It's just a cold, but when it afflicts babies under two years old, it is much more serious because their tiny airways become inflamed and they can't breathe. And it's especially serious for fragile babies who have even *smaller* airways because they were intubated for an extended period. If RSV goes untreated, it can lead to pneumonia and dire consequences. As I was learning this, I forgot that I was mad at God and thanked Him for having that on-call nurse rush us into the hospital, even though it was the last place we wanted to be.

We were quarantined to our room on the pediatric floor and had to wear yellow sterilized suits and a mask because RSV is highly contagious. I was too tired and shocked to cry.

When Dr. Julie entered our room in the early morning, I asked, "How could he possibly have gotten RSV? We barely leave the house, and I'm so careful with visitors." She calmly explained to me that RSV can come from anywhere—someone innocently touching Tim's tiny fingers or if I came home from Target and forgot to wash my hands. "But you can't beat yourself up. There is no way to know how he got it. We have to focus on his recovery," she said.

Even though Dr. Julie reassured me, I blamed myself. I was his primary caretaker, and now he was sick. Additionally, Tim's RSV symptoms scared me, in some ways more than when he was in NICU. Tim's eyes were red and swollen. His persistent coughing never stopped. And he struggled to gain his breath, which was the worst. There is nothing worse than seeing your baby gasping for air. Once I finally started crying, it was hard to stop.

Also looming in the background was that I had only one week left of maternity leave. What was I going to do if Tim needed extended time in the hospital? And my parents were supposed to come and visit us in the next few days, which had been planned to coordinate perfectly with the finale of my maternity leave. I had planned a low-key, yet fun, series of events for their trip. Now, all our plans were ruined.

Chris and I called my parents to tell them the news about Tim's RSV and how things had changed for their visit. Of course, they were sad and concerned to hear that Tim was so sick and readmitted to the hospital. But then, my dad called back about an hour later.

"Hi, Katie. It's Dad. I have some bummer news." *Oh no*, I thought. *How can there possibly be more bad news?* "Your mom can't come out West. You know how she broke her elbow when she slipped on black ice a few weeks ago? Now she has walking pneumonia too. There's no way she can take the flight. And I can't imagine they would let her on a pediatric hospital floor with pneumonia."

"I understand," I stammered through my tears.

I asked Chris if he could stay with Tim for a while because I needed an hour to myself at home. I didn't want to scream or yell about it; I wanted to be alone. Not only had I hit rock bottom of my unfulfilled expectations, now I was worried. No, I was terrified. My fragile son and my mom had a similar respiratory issue. This endless cycle of anxiety-relief-anxiety-relief was wreaking havoc on my head, heart, soul, and nervous system. As I drove home, I raged internally. *How could God do this to me? How could my life feel so fractured by these interruptions of sickness? How can I sustain the constant onslaught of unwelcome surprises?*

Now back at home in bed, the trauma and grief I'd kept at bay for over a year now was unleashed. I was angry with God because I thought God controlled all of this and accused him of being unjust. *God, I did what I was supposed to do! I would have given myself an A- or B+ for my NICU grade. And this is how I get rewarded? With more sickness. With more worry. With more unknowns.*

I see now that I thought my relationship with God was transactional—like that cosmic Santa Claus I talked about earlier. I still had the mindset *If I'm good, Cosmic Santa will put me on the "good list," and I won't get the metaphoric coal of suffering.* I sobbed in bed until I collapsed into deep sleep.

Because I was in the middle of everything still, I lacked important spiritual perspective: that suffering was not a problem to be solved but a mystery to live through. And I lacked trust. I didn't trust God's wisdom, character, or promises, even though He always came through. I didn't fully surrender to His will. I experienced moments of surrender—meeting the medical team at WRPH, during my C-section, and during most of the time in NICU. *But did I surrender because that was good stuff?* Now, in this newest wave of problems, I accused God of profound unfairness and abandonment instead of surrendering to the mystery of it and trusting in His will *especially* in the hard times.

I recently saw a woman wearing a T-shirt that summarized this paradox: "Relax, everything is out of control." One would think, by now, I would have been able to handle challenges, but my heart was still stubborn and unable to lean into the suffering.

Somehow I was able to pull myself together and go through the motions. After this deep sleep, I got up out of bed and drove back to the hospital to be with Tim and Chris because that's just what you do when you are a medical mama.

During NICU, Chris and I never stayed overnight. The intensity of the environment, the lack of sleeping accommodations, and the ratio of nurses to babies in our hospital was nearly one-to-one—all of which discourages parents from being in the hospital twenty-four-seven. But the pediatric floor is different. It serves kids from as little as Tim was, at four months, to eighteen years old. It does not have the acute care that an ICU has, so the ratio of nurses to children is quite large. Chris and I quickly realized that we had to stay overnight with Tim.

Since I was still on maternity leave and Chris had to go to work, we created a schedule in which I spent most of the nights at the hospital. Then he would spend a night so I could catch up on some sleep at home because it's nearly impossible to sleep soundly on a pediatric floor. Then I would resume being on duty at the hospital.

I hadn't felt anger or isolation like this since pregnancy. The NICU experience, while very difficult, was nurturing. There, we were surrounded by endless resources. The pediatric floor is different. But it wasn't the unit's fault that I felt stressed. I was pissed off that this was happening to us, all over again, and in a new, unfamiliar environment, even though it was the same hospital.

I took my emotions out on Dr. Julie. I was never rude or difficult with our medical team before. But here I was, demanding more attention, asking endless questions with major attitude, and wondering why Tim couldn't go home.

Tim was having so much trouble with his breathing he was relying on oxygen while they were clearing out his lungs with suction. I carefully monitored his oxygen saturation levels, which were hovering at ninety-two and ninety-three . . . not the ninety-seven or above required for discharge.

We had already spent a few days in the hospital, and there was improvement: his oxygen saturation numbers were so, so close to the normal levels. "Can't you just stop being so precise and let us go home? He's close enough!" I begged her.

But Dr. Julie wouldn't budge. She would not round up. Tim had to reach the official numbers to be allowed home. I knew that I was being very difficult—taking out my anger and frustration on her—which was not like me. I didn't like the person I was becoming, but the anger was consuming me, and it had to go somewhere.

Dr. Julie absorbed my anger and continued to do her job. She is such an ethical, responsible doctor and would not round up on Tim's stats, no matter how much I protested. And she was right in her assessment. We would later discover that Tim had a secondary complication, and if we hadn't been in the hospital, we might not have caught it as quickly.

Then my dad arrived, and on the pediatric floor, on the fourth day of Tim's stay, Dad could feel my hostile energy in the room as soon as he entered. "Katie, this is life. Do not worry a minute about the expectations for this trip. Tim is sick. We could not control that. We must love and support him. You must accept this situation. Tim is a medically fragile baby. You have to learn to accept that his path is more complicated. You must accept this situation," he said gently. *You must accept this situation.* I clung to those words.

I really thought that our discharge of NICU was the finish line. But this RSV situation showed me that Chris and I really did have a challenging road with a baby like Tim. With a medically complicated kid, there is no official finish line.

That's why my dad had to come to me: to soften my heart, dissipate my despair and anger, and plant a seed of hope. God was sending me gentle strength through my dad, but I was unable to see it at the time. Dad also told me, "You really should apologize to Dr. Julie. She's an excellent doctor, and you are treating her like crap."

Again, it was very wise advice. I apologized to Dr. Julie and brought her a gift. I felt so badly about the way I treated her and wanted her to know my genuine contrition. Dr. Julie was touched by my gesture, and we ended up being great friends.

Tim recovered from RSV. His cough subsided, and his breathing became stronger. But as I was changing his diaper, day after day, in our room, I noticed that he had a strange, tumor-like growth on his tummy. I brought it to the attention of our inpatient care team, and they confirmed my suspicions that it looked strange. One of the doctors on rotation took a black Sharpie marker and drew a circle around the strange, bubble-like growth. Over the course of a day or two, the growth expanded beyond the boundaries of the thick black line. It was getting worse by the day; it was inflamed, bright red, and "angry looking," as one doctor said.

The infectious disease team was called in.

Now, this was before COVID and not many people knew what an infectious disease doctor was. I was fixated on this title: *infectious disease doctor*. "Infectious disease? What is going on? How is this even the name of a doctor?" I asked Dr. Julie. This was not good.

She understood my confusion and fear. "Yes, that's the name of the specialty. We are wondering if Tim's Gore-Tex patch has an infection." When Tim had his closure surgery on day seven of NICU, the muscles weren't large enough to attach, so they used an internal Gore-Tex patch to secure his muscle closure. Using a Gore-Tex patch or other synthetic material is a common practice for surgery, and some people live their entire lives with these foreign materials in their bodies. But there is always the risk that the material can get infected.

If I was scared when Tim had RSV, I was now in a complete state of panic. Infection is serious and nebulous territory. I thought of MRSA and sepsis and how they come on quickly and forcefully. I feared that the infection would spread from his patch to his blood . . . from there my thoughts were spiraling.

The ID team swooped upon our room. Sometimes there were three or four doctors at a time examining Tim and this expanding, tumor-like growth. It felt like the ID team had more questions than answers, and it was a giant game of which came first: the RSV or the infection? Did the RSV cause the infection because Tim's overall immune system was so weak? Was the entire patch infected? Could they wash the patch with an antibiotic and leave it in? Would Tim have to endure another surgery and have the patch removed and replaced with a new patch? Never in our journey did we have so much uncertainty, and the weight of these unknowns nearly broke me at times.

But a few things were certain or near certain. Tim was extremely agitated and uncomfortable. Next, they were confident that the patch was infected; it had a slime-like film covering it. The ID team decided to administer a regime of intense antibiotics over the course of the next few weeks and observe Tim carefully. The team at the hospital also decided that it would be best to discharge Tim because there was a chance that he could develop a secondary infection if he stayed in the hospital too long. The team decided I was responsible enough to administer the antibiotics through a central line.

I wanted so desperately to go home because the pediatric floor was a difficult lifestyle—if one could call it a lifestyle—to endure. The lack of sleep, the high ratio of patients to nurses, and the huge range of ages was less nurturing than NICU, and my confidence wavered in this environment. Fear was my primary emotion on the pediatric floor, and it was a breathless, manic panic that I hadn't felt since the early days of the pregnancy.

But I felt torn. I was terrified to administer through a central line all by myself. A central line is a catheter placed into a large vein. It was placed in Tim's femoral vein, dangling just below his groin. The purpose of a central line was to deliver long-term, intravenous antibiotics to Tim so the infection in his tummy would go away. But it has a lot of risk; if the central line is not kept sterile, it can lead to other infections, like staph. The central line was close to his diaper, and I had to maintain a completely sterile environment. Yes, I was a responsible parent, but I wasn't a doctor or nurse. The weight of this burden felt too much. *What if I don't administer the antibiotic properly? What if I don't flush the line correctly? What if bacteria gets into the wound area?* In theory, I could kill my baby doing any one of these processes incorrectly.

The infectious disease team had me come to their office and taught me how to administer the antibiotic as well as how to flush the central line and keep it clean. I have never watched, studied, took more notes, or watched more videos with such careful attention ever in my life. In other parts of our hospital journey, I had a light-hearted approach to my learning. Here, I was studying for what I thought was the life of our child because I actually had to implement the solution myself. I had a laser-like focus. I felt driven in a different way than the determination I had felt during the pregnancy; this was a focus rooted in fear, anger, and exhaustion. I didn't want to do any of this, I had negative energy about it, I was completely fatigued physically and emotionally—but I didn't have a choice. I had to accomplish my mission.

And, I had to go back to work in three days.

How can I possibly go back to work with this huge responsibility? But even more, I wondered how I would go back to work, pretend this all wasn't happening, and function at a reasonable level. I had thrown out the idea of achievement at work; now, I just wanted to survive. It was back to work, part two, and it was worse than part one when I'd had to return while Tim was in NICU.

I was living a modern mom's version of Job. Like Job, it was one horrible thing after another, suffering without end, and ceaseless laments to God of injustice. Life was exhausting and agonizing—a grind that seemed never-ending, slow-going, and isolating. I dreamed of a giant *fast forward* button for my own life. I needed to see ahead, see if this grind would last forever, if things would get better, or if our lives would be endless hospital visits with little time for a social life and friends. *Will I live a life of constant lament? Will I ever have days of fun, joy, peace, and gratitude? Will I be blessed with abundance at the end of my trials, like Job was?* It just didn't seem possible that there would be a happy ending.

Where were God and Mary? I felt ghosted by someone I thought to be a dear friend. And so began the Dark Ages of my relationship with God.

Because I felt ghosted, I responded accordingly. I decided to dump, unfriend, and block God first and turned to myself instead. I was done with Him. I didn't want to pray or talk to Him. I would muddle through this on my own. I decided to use contemporary, New Age methods instead. Now, I see this reliance on my self-determination was a mistake and the hallmark of arrogance, but I thought I could go it alone. Little did I know that things would get (way) worse and this tipping point of unknown infection proved to be instrumental in building the endurance to keep on keeping on. So, while I unfriended God, He never left my side.

I knew that my heart was turning to stone and that my bitterness and anger were at an all-time high, so I made the conscious decision to be outwardly positive at all costs, driven by sheer willpower. I didn't want to be a person who would always see the dark side of things, ruin someone else's good mood by reminding them of my misery, or be demanding to doctors, nurses, and friends. It was like being on an extremely restrictive diet without understanding the root of the problem. I made a choice, then and there, that I would be positive no matter what. No matter how hard it was to be so. No matter how much of an act it was.

Tim was discharged, and I was convinced it was because of my new positive attitude and wishful thinking. Dad went home to Massachusetts and left me with more wisdom: "Katie, you can do this. You are a smart, strong woman. Don't let the central line or work or anything scare you."

I called Mike and his boss, Kyle, to explain my situation. "Mike, Kyle, I'm in a bad spot. Tim has developed a serious infection and we've been back in the hospital for the past two weeks. They decided it would be best if he came home while we administered some heavy-duty antibiotics to him through a central line. But it takes two people to give the medicine. One person has to hold Tim down and the other to deliver the medicine. And we have to do it three times a day. It's serious stuff because it's a central line and I've spent the past week taking nursing classes to learn how to do it. And we need careful observation of the infection as well as his behavior. So . . . can I work from home instead of coming into the office?"

They didn't even hesitate. "Yes, Katie. Work from home."

My mother-in-law, Susan, who lived locally, would help me administer the central line and watch Tim while I worked. And once a week, I took little Tim, with the central line dangling off him, into the ID office (which mostly serves adult patients) so they could check on the infection and the condition of the central line. We got into a good groove.

Life went on like this for a month. The routine calmed my nerves and eased my fears. I was tethered to our condo by that central line. It was hardly perfect, but things stayed afloat—my marriage, my son's health, and work. Our social life had taken a hit, along with our innocence, but we kept going, trying to get as much rest and sleep as we could. The positive attitude fueled by discipline was working: we weren't going to let this infection or central line or the new routine get us down. We dealt with our situation, day by day, and developed a more optimistic outlook and confidence that Tim would heal.

CHAPTER 15

Stop!

Amonth after the development of the infection, Dr. Shapiro's team, the pediatric surgeons, wanted to examine Tim. The "angry tummy" looked a little less angry, but the tumor-like quality was still there. It looked like the bumpy back of a toad. Though I didn't want to admit it, I knew the infection was lingering.

The surgeon on rotation that day was Dr. Moreau. Dr. Moreau hadn't been a part of Tim's regular care team, but the entire surgical staff were rock stars, so I didn't have any worries about her checking Tim. Perhaps her eye would be just the outside perspective we needed.

"Have you been doing the antibiotic through the central line for a month?" she asked.

"Yes, it's been a month," I replied.

"This is nowhere close to being healed. And it looks like a huge abscess." And with that, she reached for a tool to lance what she thought was an abscess.

Out of nowhere, I roared, "*STOP!*"

She dropped her tools.

"PLEASE DON'T! We don't know if it's an infection or a hernia or anything. Do an ultrasound before you do anything!"

I truly don't know where the inner roar came from. I trusted these doctors implicitly. I had the utmost respect for this surgical team because they had saved my baby boy. But a force bigger than me (the Holy Spirit?) took over my whole being and stopped her from performing a small surgical procedure that may have had terrible consequences—like lancing a critical organ.

"You are right, Katie. We need an ultrasound. But here's the news you really don't want to hear: We need to admit Tim again."

I thought the appointment would be a simple check-in and then I would go home to stay the course. After all, I was going to ID once a week and no one had said anything. Now we were being admitted back to the hospital? I was in disbelief, thrown overboard into choppy waters without a radar, rudderless, adrift in fear and confusion. *Why don't these doctors know what's going on? Who is the leader here? Why am I telling doctors to stop? Who do I think I am? And where are God and*

Mary—even though I am over them anyway? Have they jumped this awful ship of uncertainty too?

Chris was furious when he heard the news that we were being readmitted. "We need bags? You have already admitted Tim to the hospital? These people are incompetent. How is this happening? I thought you were just going in for a check-up. How are you back at the hospital?"

"Chris, I know," I responded through tears. "It turns out that the infection is still there. And they need to do an ultrasound and more tests and observations here in the hospital. Please, just get the bags."

"No. This is insane. We need a second opinion. They have no clue what they are doing over there. We are back and forth and back and forth. And you are chained to our condo because of giving medicine through a *central line* when you aren't even a nurse. What kind of insane expectation and responsibility are they putting on you? This is ridiculous. No, we need to get a second opinion somewhere else."

I agreed with everything that Chris said, except the part about a second opinion. Like him, I was frustrated and angry with the doctors and nurses, but I couldn't imagine starting all over again at a new hospital with potentially different strategies. And most importantly, a new hospital didn't know Tim. I didn't think it was wise to change care plans and teams this late in the game when my gut instinct trusted our team at Western Regional Pediatric Hospital.

It was the first ever disagreement we had about Tim's care plan. Chris reluctantly agreed to stay at WRPH. I can't remember how many days we were back in the hospital for observations because those days blurred together from fear and lack of sleep. But there was one thing about this time period that was distinct.

It was Mother's Day, and I was stuck in the hospital. But I was too exhausted to grieve the loss of my very first Mother's Day. There wasn't brunch or cards or flowers. I don't even have pictures, only vague memories of the day. I recall that I wanted a mimosa, but I can't remember if that simple desire was fulfilled. Though this day sounds sad, I was too exhausted to care.

Chris and I were relieved when Dr. Shapiro entered the picture again after being away on vacation. He met with us immediately.

"I heard you all were back. I heard that you have had a horrible month. I am sorry that I was gone," he apologized to us.

I was stunned—a world-class surgeon was apologizing to us about taking a vacation. The color came back to my face.

We trusted Dr. Shapiro, it was important for us to have a familiar face, and most importantly, Dr. Shapiro had a plan.

"We are going to remove this patch. And there are three possible outcomes and I will tell them in order of best to worst case. First, we remove the patch and his muscles are big enough for me to attach. This is best-case because it will mean that there are no foreign bodies in his body, and you won't have to see me again. Second, we remove the patch and put in another patch. But I won't do Gore-Tex. I will select a different patch in the hopes he will tolerate it better. Third, I scrub the patch clean, keep it in for now, and we take it out when he's big enough to reattach the muscles."

Yes! A plan! After all this time—after about five weeks of infection inertia—we finally had a plan. I embraced Dr. Shapiro. I couldn't help myself. For all this time, the fear of the unknown, the feeling of being tossed overboard with no life raft, consumed me. But now that we had a plan—with Dr. Shapiro leading—my faith in the doctors was restored.

I asked him two things: "What do you think is the most realistic possibility?" and "When is this surgery happening?"

Dr. Shapiro replied, "I think I will take out the patch and replace it with another. Tim is only five months old, so I can't tell, until I go in, how big his muscles are. And the surgery will happen today."

It was unbelievable that the surgery was happening so quickly, but the past five weeks had felt like an academic exercise in developing hypotheses as to why my baby had a huge, angry, tumor-like growth on his tummy; I was ready to move onto the more decisive and action-based specialty that is surgery. Let's do this! I felt my old self reawakening.

The surgery lasted about one hour, much shorter than we expected. Chris and I hung out in the waiting room. He worked while I just chatted with my in-laws. I wasn't nervous. I wasn't scared. I knew this nightmare would finally be over. I was slowly leaning into the realization that there would never be a finish line for a child like Tim, but at least we could move out of the horrible inertia of infection.

Dr. Shapiro successfully removed Tim's patch and attached his muscles—the best possible outcome and, truly, beyond my expectations. "It's done. I took out the patch, and I was able to attach his muscles. You can head over to the pediatric floor for recovery," Dr. Shapiro announced.

I embraced Dr. Shapiro, for the second time that day. "Thank you, Dr. Shapiro. Just thank you." Chris went over to him, and they firmly shook hands.

When he closed Tim's stomach muscles, Dr. Shapiro also closed this miserable chapter of RSV, infection, central line, and pediatric floor. Though I had shut out God, I now know, that He was present with us—through my inner roar and through Dr. Shapiro's wise assessment and skillful, successful surgery. Now we could focus on our small family and work, enjoy some baby milestones, and experience our first summer together.

Summer proved to be just that and more. We did things that families do, like go to restaurants while onlookers cooed about how adorable our baby was, go to the lake for a little beach day, and take Tim for hikes in the glorious western outdoors. We finally had the luxury of worrying about trivial things like putting on enough sunscreen, getting home in time for naps, and if we'd packed enough formula for a day trip. It was the first time I felt like an innocent, carefree mom consumed with *easy* worries since those few weeks in between Chris's shingles and Tim's RSV diagnosis.

The end of May and the entire month of June were glorious months of no medical or hospital activity. We had calm and peace in our home environment. Tim was sleeping more and more throughout the night. I felt refreshed when I went to work. Chris and I were getting along beautifully. And we started to observe Tim's little, non-medical milestones: getting a mouthful of teeth and starting to eat solid foods.

While I knew that my faith was compromised, and I was aware that I had an ocean of trauma, that summer I felt many moments of joy and finally some peace. I didn't want to pray. I didn't want to think. I didn't want to worry. I wanted to enjoy every second of our trivial worries and newfound peace. I also wanted some sleep and was finally able to catch up on that.

We even traveled that summer. We visited Chris's extended family in Missouri and introduced Tim to his great-grandmother and great-aunts where he was doted upon. And then, we went to Boston to see my parents and for Tim to meet my huge extended family. We had his baptism at my home parish when he was exactly six months old. His baptism was a beautiful event, and it stirred feelings of holiness in me, but I still was in my one-sided, dark time with God.

It wasn't until I recounted the baptism to one of my friends, who said, "Katie, what a blessed event. You know—the greatest gift we can give our children is the gift of faith" that a little spark lit up in me for the first time in weeks.

CHAPTER 16
The Condo

And then serenity came to a screeching halt, yet again. It was the middle of July and we were at a party thrown by our friend, Cynthia, who had introduced Chris and I to one another. Chris took me aside during the party. "Have you read your email?"

"No, I'm not checking my phone. What's up?"

"Sean and Kathy are selling the condo." Sean and Kathy were our landlords whom we'd been renting from because we were both relatively new to the area and wanted to know the neighborhoods better before we jumped into home owner-ship. But, as we were now learning, this was the risk of being a renter.

Sean and Kathy had originally offered us a two-year lease, but at the last second they changed the contract and told us,

"We just switched it, so it's a one-year lease, but we hope you'll live here as long as you want. Two years, five years—we want this to be your home." However, during the actual rental process, we ran into roadblock after roadblock with them; I should have known their words were hollow.

Nevertheless, we'd made the condo our home. It was our respite in the middle of all the chaos. It was the place of our homecoming. Tim's adorable nursery was in this condo. A lightning bolt of shock rippled through my body, and my thoughts went into dizzying overdrive, catastrophizing the situation. *What are we going to do? Where are we going to live? Do they have a clue what we have been through? Can't they just give us a few months to settle, to allow Tim's health to stabilize, and then sell the condo? Where should we move? How am I going to find a clean, safe rental so Tim can thrive? What about the wait list for day care in our current neighborhood?*

Sean and Kathy had every right to sell their condo, but they *knew* we were just out of NICU. They *knew* Tim was a medically fragile baby. And they still did the crappy thing. While all of this was happening, we maintained our responsibility: we were always on time with rent and never complained about problems in the condo. It made me realize that a lot of people don't get it. Even though Sean and Kathy knew we were going through a difficult time, they didn't empathize or sympathize about our experience. They just wanted the rent paid on time.

Chris and I tried to tell them our challenges without sounding like victims, but our efforts were in vain. "Can we please extend the lease for six more months? Just until Tim's health stabilizes and we have a bit more time to look for a new rental?" They responded with a firm no. They even tried to sell the condo to us, but we knew the quirks and shortcomings of the property and weren't interested.

I had never wished bad things on anyone during our entire journey, but now I wanted to egg Sean and Kathy's house. I know, I know—how immature and un-Christian. But they sucked. Egging their house would have been very gratifying.

I realized, after all, that this was not life or death, as our other past issues had been. But for some reason, that gave me little comfort. I was fixated on how Sean, but mostly Kathy, were two of the most awful, greedy people on the planet, how they *emailed* us the difficult news instead of calling us, and how they completely uprooted us from the only stability we had. Perhaps it's easier to have a real-life bogeyman—or in this case, bogeywoman—instead of all the unknown demons in one's head. And sure enough, Sean and Kathy became the external objects on whom I could take out all my anger and frustration.

One night, after Tim went to bed, Chris and I sat on our small front porch and brainstormed what our next steps would be. "We have three options. Option A is that we move in with your parents so that we have time to make a sound decision. Option B is that we find another rental in this neighborhood. And Option C is that we buy this condo."

Chris quickly responded to Option B. "Let's start apartment hunting." But Option B was my least favorite option. I had searched for months and months for this current condo and felt lucky that we found it.

"I don't want to do Option B. It took me forever to find this place. We need the sure thing. My first choice is Option A: to live with your parents while we figure this out."

I was exhausted, stressed, anxious, and risk averse. I needed the sure thing, the safe thing. First, Chris's parents' home was big, clean, and beautiful. Second, Susan and Dave had been watching Tim while Chris and I worked until we could enroll Tim in day care, so this way, they would no longer have a commute to our current condo. And last, I thought, if we lived in the Boston area, we would live with my parents in a heartbeat while we figured out our next steps. Why would this be any different?

Chris did not like this idea. "Katie, no. We cannot live with my parents. I don't think you understand that it is not emotionally healthy for us as a new family. No, not an option."

I understood his rationale, but I simply couldn't move from rental to rental with a medically fragile kid in tow, putting him on a different day care wait list every year. What if the next rental pulled the same crap? What if we had to move again the following year? I needed stability. I needed a quiet, healthy home. I needed the sure thing. I needed time to think. I needed the practical option, but I didn't want to buy the condo. I knew we would outgrow the condo within a year or two, and it had all sorts of annoying quirks. So, I steadfastly stuck to Option A. "Chris, I can't move again. I can't. And we can't quite afford the house that we want right now. We need to go practical. We need to move in with your parents."

After a few days, Chris agreed. We packed up our stuff, Sean and Kathy stiffed us on part of the security deposit, and we moved to Chris's parents' home, about forty-five minutes from where we were living.

I didn't end up egging Sean and Kathy's house. But I really wanted to.

We moved in the middle of September when Tim was eight months old and doing very well. He had a typical routine of eat, play, sleep, as well as some nontypical appointments with a physical therapist, occupational therapist, and visits with all his different specialists, such as GI. Chris and I were commuting to work and trying to adjust to living in someone else's home.

Susan and Dave, my in-laws, had a large home. So, we were physically comfortable, but we were not emotionally restful. It is true that it is difficult to adjust to four adults living in one home. It was like having the action, excitement, and community of having roommates, while trying to maintain the boundaries of our own little family unit.

I realized, quickly, thanks to my dad, that boundaries in this environment would be challenging. "Katie, throw that idea of boundaries out the window until you guys find your own place. If you lived with us, it would be the same way. Just accept the situation and know that it will be temporary." And for the most part, I adopted this sage philosophy. It was harder for Chris to take on this mindset because they were his parents, but he managed.

We didn't plan on being at Susan and Dave's forever, so we began house-hunting quickly. Then, Susan mentioned a new neighborhood in the western suburbs, called Canyon Ranch. "You need to check this neighborhood out. They are doing new construction and the neighborhood has a ton of amenities." I was set on being in a more metropolitan area and not the suburbs, but we decided to check it out.

Canyon Ranch was everything and more. Though it looked like a suburb in Arizona, which clashed with my New England aesthetic, it had all the qualities that we were looking for: there were already over eight hundred homes, tons of kids, sidewalks, a gorgeous community pool, open areas, playgrounds, great schools, and friendly neighbors. And most importantly, the new homes were modern, beautiful, and within our price range.

We put down earnest money for a lot within the week.

CHAPTER 17

Miracle Mary

If we zoom out and all at once look at September 2014 to September 2015, finding about the omphalocele diagnosis at the twenty-week appointment to now, I would never, ever, in a million years, have been able to imagine that all this drama and life-changing events would happen to Chris and me so quickly and so intensely. Usually, when people have a nine-month-old, they are happy to create a reasonable schedule, celebrate their baby's milestones, and perhaps start thinking about growing their family. But consider what had had happened for us in the past year:

∞ Tim received omphalocele diagnosis; we waited for news of genetic abnormalities.

∞ We experienced a pregnancy with a rare fetal diagnosis.

∞ I delivered baby and was not able to hold him at birth.

∞ We stayed in NICU for two months, which included three surgeries.

∞ Chris got shingles.

∞ Tim got RSV.

∞ Tim has a severe infection in his abdomen.

∞ Tim was discharged from the hospital, and I administered antibiotics through a central line.

∞ Tim had surgery to remove the root cause of the infection (surgery number four).

∞ We moved in with in-laws because our rental was being sold.

∞ Days after our move into my in-laws', we bought a lot to build a new home.

I look at this list and think, *How could this possibly have all happened within one year?* but it did, and we had little control over it. If we could endure all those things in a year, surely, we could just coast through living with our in-laws, watch Tim grow and thrive, and design our new home. We were hoping and praying that life would be on the upswing now. The medical procedures and issues seemed to be a thing of the past. And now, we could focus on our exciting future as a new family building their dream home. Finally, things seemed to be coming together. This would be the fun part! All the chaos and trauma of the past year seemed firmly in the rear-view. We were moving onward!

Once again, I was wrong.

One night, Chris, Tim, and I were invited to our friends' home for a vegan meal and to see their new house, constructed by the same builders as ours. We had a wonderful time. But when we got home, Tim vomited bright-yellow liquid all over the foyer.

"Oh my gosh, what's going on? He was fine at dinner," I exclaimed. We cleaned up the mess. But Tim continued to vomit for the next fifteen minutes. And he would not stop crying. Susan, Chris, Dave, and I all took turns trying to soothe Tim, but nothing worked.

The crying lasted for hours. And the more Tim cried, the more us adults blamed one another. What started as bewilderment, moved onto worry, then onto blaming. "You said it was a vegan meal. Maybe they had honey in one of the dishes? Did you let him have honey? Babies can't have honey," Dave asked.

It was a weird question to ask, but it was what we all latched onto. Even though it was late, I called Evan, the host, and asked him about the honey. "No. There wasn't honey in the meal. I'm sorry Tim is so sick." Meanwhile, Chris was furious about this honey issue and felt that we were being blamed by his father for being bad parents. It got tense. It got heated. Finally, Chris broke through the chaos and declared that we should take Tim to the ER.

This time, we decided not to return to Western Regional Pediatric Hospital. First, we were still smarting from the experience we'd had on the pediatric floor back in May when it took so long to get a final diagnosis for the infection. Second, Susan and Dave lived closer to a different hospital, so we drove to their ER. The choice of hospitals was a significant decision because it led to a few misdiagnoses by the new doctors who didn't know Tim.

As we drove, the fear and trauma resurfaced for me. So much that, when we got there, I had to excuse myself during the admittance process because I was crying so hard. One common theme in Tim's medical trials was that I was unable to participate in the admittance process. I don't know what it was, but I just couldn't do it, and Chris has to be the strong, brave one to hold Tim and take care of all the questions and paperwork. Tim was admitted to the ER, and the doctors began to examine him.

"It looks like he's just sick. Bad stomach bug. Here's some Zofran to curb the nausea. Just try to feed him ice chips and small amounts of formula so he stays hydrated. Watch his diapers to make sure they are wet."

Nothing was wrong, they explained. We were discharged.

Now, I started to second-guess my intuition. This baby was screaming and wailing for hours. He couldn't keep anything down. But it was normal baby GI/flu/bug stuff, they'd said. It puzzled me. Tim had quieted down and looked sleepy, so maybe it was just a bug and we were overreacting due to the trauma we had been through over the past year.

Chris and I barely slept that night but got up the next morning to go to work. Susan watched Tim during the day while we were at work. When I came home from the office, Susan was sitting outside with Tim, who was limp and lethargic. "Katie, something is wrong. He has been lethargic like this all day. There is no sparkle in his eye."

I didn't know what to do. "Should I bring him to the pediatrician? The ER insisted it was a bug."

"Katie, bring him to the pediatrician. This is more than a bug."

Our pediatrician, though not our primary pediatrician, was able to see Tim right away. Chris and I explained the symptoms, but we received the same diagnosis as the night before. "Chris and Katie, I know you have been through a lot. But this is a normal baby thing, not the intense issues that you experienced in the past year. Just keep him hydrated with his formula and he will perk up within a day or two." We were released from that appointment with the same diagnosis—a simple stomach virus—but also, the same lethargic baby.

By this time, it had been about thirty-six hours since Tim had vomited the bright-yellow substance, yet he was still unable to eat. And he had no energy. He was usually an active, happy baby. Something was wrong.

The next day, Tim vomited bright-green bile, even though he had not eaten for a while. He was barely moving. We decided to go to the closest ER (still not Western Regional Pediatric Hospital) for the second time in three days. It felt like Groundhog Day. We pulled up, got out, I sobbed uncontrollably, Chris admitted Tim to the ER, and Tim was examined. But this time, things took a more serious and somber tone.

"Tim had an omphalocele at birth? How many abdominal surgeries did he have? What color was the vomit?"

I replied, "Yes, we were here the other day and we told you the other day he had an omphalocele. He has had three major abdominal surgeries: silo, skin closure, and muscle closure. The vomit was bright yellow, like Big Bird. And then, this afternoon, it was bright green."

"We need to do an ultrasound. It sounds like he has a bowel obstruction."

As the mother of a baby with an omphalocele, I should have known more about bowel obstruction. I should have known that multiple surgeries create scar tissue, and scar tissue can cause obstruction. I should have known that brightly colored vomit was an indicator of a bowel obstruction. And it was said to me, after the fact, that our surgical team should have warned me about the likelihood of bowel obstructions. But at the time, I didn't know anything about them.

The ER team called in the Flight for Life team to transport Tim to WRPH by helicopter. "We think it's best if he is treated there because they know him, and the surgeons know his anatomy, since all his surgeries were performed there."

Terror.

My baby boy was being transported to another hospital via emergency helicopter. It was beyond comprehension. Until this point, I believed that the infection inertia was our lowest low, our scariest trial. But now we were having, by far, a *lowest, lowest low*. And it wasn't just a low; it was terrifying, adrenaline-filled, electrical, five alarm fire disaster. They pulled out an adult-sized gurney, and my tiny baby was strapped down on it, wailing, reaching for me, as six Air Life team members, in their blue air suits, were preparing to transport us. I was hysterical. But my terror was only making Tim more scared. Then the medical team decided to change the mode of transport from helicopter to ambulance, but we still had the acute care team in the ambulance with us. This took my terror level down slightly. One parent was allowed in the ambulance, and we decided I would go with Tim while Chris would drive to WRPH on his own.

The captain of the group on the ambulance, John, was unruffled, professional, and exceptional at keeping a state of equilibrium and calm. "Mrs. McCarty, we are a team of medical professionals with the backgrounds of ICU nurses and doctors. Many of us come from military backgrounds and are able to perform procedures at any time, even during this transport, if we need to. You are in the best hands possible, and if this were my child, I would be relieved to have my team there for his medical needs. If we need to perform a procedure right now, we have all the experience and equipment in this ambulance to do it. You are in the best hands possible."

I believed him. I had faith in him. In fact, years later, when my sons and I were having ice cream in Andover, Massachusetts, and saw a Flight Life crew in blue jump suits—and obviously, not the crew who helped us—come into the shop, I couldn't help but go up to them to express my gratitude for what they do.

I calmed down from my hysteria to a place of stillness. Then, John asked me about Tim, our family, and eventually shifted the conversation to dinner-party small talk, like where I was from and what I did for a living. By the time we reached WRPH, I was in a serene place of mind and better prepared to handle the next phase of hospital tumult.

Months later, one of our outpatient doctors, after hearing this dramatic story, said, "Are you serious? That ER released you back to Western practically via airlift? Do you realize this is like a Republican campaign lending their jet to a Democratic nominee to get to an event? This never happens. Too many egos. Boy, you guys must be special people." We were hardly special people, but I think that once the pieces were put together, everyone knew that this poor little baby was in serious condition and something had to be done urgently. Again, I didn't have the perspective that I do now, but in order for something this extraordinary to happen, it had to be bigger than us. Spoiler alert: It was God, again.

Back at our home base, WRPH, the terror was still there, but there was a smidge of relief—we were where everyone knew us and knew Tim's story and anatomy. Of course, it wasn't a typical homecoming of big hugs and cheers, it was a weary relief that we knew where the soda machines, restrooms, and nurse stations were. And I wish that I had more gratitude than that. It sounds ungrateful that that was our only comfort, but after months of all the trauma and exhaustion of life in and out of the hospital, that's all the optimism and gratitude we could muster. It was "Wow! They added Orange Fanta to the soda machine," not "We are back home where our son's life was saved many times over."

The ultrasound at WRPH confirmed that Tim had had a bowel obstruction for the past four days. At the time, I didn't realize how frustrated I should have been that there were two misdiagnoses. Perhaps the exhaustion of it all was a blessing so I could focus on the present situation and not waste time Monday-morning-quarterbacking.

The short-term plan was to drain his system. They would put an NG tube down his nose and suction all the gunk out of his GI system for at least twenty-four hours. During this time, he would be on morphine to ease the pain and let his tiny body relax during the suction. They reassured us that this was the best first course of action. They would evaluate the situation after twenty-four hours. Chris and I had faith in this team and went with the plan.

I can't exactly recall how little sleep Chris and I had gotten during this hazy time of the bowel obstruction. But we had been dealing with this mysterious ailment for about four days. So, it meant that we hadn't slept more than a few hours at a time during these four days. My in-laws insisted that we go back to house after our first night at the hospital to get some quality sleep, a hot shower, and a few more of our things. They would watch Tim at the hospital. Chris and I left the hospital around nine a.m. because we felt that everything was stable enough for us to leave for a few hours to rest. Susan and Dave were up to speed with the situation, and they would watch Tim while we were gone. Additionally and importantly, we loved our new nurse, Sonja, who would be on shift for the day—another reason we felt comfortable leaving. She was bright, competent, and nurturing. Chris and I said our goodbyes, and sure enough, we slept hard at my in-laws' house.

We both got up around one p.m. and slowly made our way to the hospital. It's hard to describe the exhaustion—physical and mental—that we felt and how it truly slows down the body. I suppose it's like when I used to run marathons; you want to move faster but know that if you do speed up, your body will cramp and seize, and you won't be able to complete the race. Chris and I had the good sense to pace ourselves and moved slowly to the hospital because we knew that we had to be alert to learn more about Tim's current status and make decisions.

When we arrived at the hospital, we saw that a new nurse was in our room, along with Susan and Dave. I asked the new nurse, "Where's Sonja?"

"The floor is only half full today, so she was sent home because there weren't enough patients. My name is Mary, and I will be your nurse for the rest of the day. Nice to meet you guys."

I was angry. I loved Sonja. I trusted Sonja. Why was there a new nurse in our room? This never happened. In all our time at the hospital, we never experienced a nurse leaving mid-shift. And I was just so tired—tired of all the misdiagnoses, tired of the red tape at hospitals, tired of changes, tired of everything. I'm not sure how I came across, but I snipped back, "That's weird. We've been in the hospital a lot and this has never happened. We really liked Sonja. But, oh well. We're here now. Can you get us up to date?" I have many flaws, but I am not a passive aggressive person. But on this day, I was at peak passive aggressiveness.

Mary paused as she was getting herself up to speed on Tim's situation. Susan and Dave, probably feeling the tension, excused themselves from the room. "I'm still learning about everything. But I just can't believe all that you have gone through. They told me about the omphalocele and all your time in NICU and the complications. I can't even imagine how hard this must be. I have two sons, and I really can't imagine having to deal with all that you have dealt with."

Now, I was furious. *Why is she acting like a therapist with me right now? Why is she giving me all this sympathy? And is all this sympathy a cover for her incompetence?* I didn't need a hug; I needed answers and solutions for my son's current state. *Why did they let Sonja go home and now I have her?* I don't know if it was the exhaustion or despair of the situation, but my mind was in an incensed state, and I was fearful that I was going to say something I would later regret so I kept my mouth tightly shut.

Instead, I asked, "What is the course of action? We've only been gone a few hours, but I know we are hitting the twenty-four-hour mark of the suction and I want to know what's next."

Mary looked at Tim's chart, studied it for a while. "It looks like he's up for another round of morphine. But . . ."

"But—WHAT?" I snapped.

She hemmed and hawed. "I don't know. This doesn't seem right. For the morphine schedule that he is on, he should be a more active baby. But he looks lethargic and out of it. I don't know. Do you know when his last dose of morphine was? Oh, wait—it was around eight a.m. No, this isn't right. I am looking at him, and I can't give him more morphine in his current state."

Now I became terrified. And Chris did, too. Though, his reaction was less of anger and more of a confused, exhausted state. To me, she seemed indecisive. She seemed incompetent. She seemed to be thinking out loud. And I said as much. "We just took a four-hour break from here, and you guys are supposed to know what to do and what his next steps are. You are the medical professionals, not us. We don't know what to do. This seems like there was a communication break-down. And I'm so tired that I can barely stand up. Please, please, please—figure this out. Get the doctor in here." I couldn't believe how rude and demanding I was being, but I was panicking. The situation seemed unsupervised and chaotic. And when I looked down at Tim in his crib, Mary was right: Tim was completely lethargic.

Mary's gut and professional instincts were correct. "I cannot administer more morphine to this baby. He is barely breathing. We need to re-evaluate his status. If I give him more morphine, he will code. I will be right back," Mary explained.

And she dashed out of the room. My panic level, on a scale from zero to ten, was at a fifteen.

Did she just say that Tim would code? Oh Lord, did she really just say "code"? I was horrified. Panicked. Coding meant that Tim, my baby, could stop breathing. Now I was hysterical. We had been through a lot with Tim, but we never heard the possibility that he would code and have to be brought back to life.

I started pacing wildly like a trapped animal in the cramped room, and Chris embraced me in a giant bear hug. But I needed to be moving, to be *in action*, to will an actual action, *a decision*, to be made. I began talking to myself out loud, "We just came back to the hospital after a short break, and now we have a crisis? A serious crisis. This is worse than NICU. How could things be worse than NICU?" I was processing in real time. My usual self-control was gone. Everything, including me, was a chaotic mess.

I hadn't reached out to God since the infection, but now I begged for Him. I begged Him to come back to me, to intervene, so that Tim would not code.

A team of medical professionals swooped into our room. They were openly debating Tim's status and the next course of action. Mary was adamant that Tim was at risk for cardio-pulmonary arrest—which meant he would stop breathing—if she administered more morphine. But the assigned doctor,

Dr. Anderson, stood firm on his assessment to continue the drainage with morphine doses. I was becoming even more hysterical because I was voiceless as this heated discussion ensued.

Dr. Anderson, our primary doctor for the day, responded, "No. Keep him on this schedule. It's just been twenty-four hours of the suction. We need to continue suction for a few more hours and monitor him. This happens. Keep his schedule. Keep suctioning. We aren't doing surgery right now."

But Mary was firm in her assessment. "No. This baby cannot sustain this schedule. Kerry"—she turned to the hospitalist—"he needs surgery. Escalate this. Now. Get Dr. Sideris in here now."

Nurse Mary was going over Dr. Anderson's head to the surgeon in front of him. I could see the smoke rising out of his ears. But as she was advocating her position, I thought to myself, *She is right. And Dr. Anderson is wrong.* It was also at this moment that I realized I was completely wrong about Mary. *She entered into our lives at exactly the right—and critical— moment.* The weird shift change, her persistent questioning, her quick thinking, and her gut reactions were all spot on.

Mother Mary was with us, here and now, through Nurse Mary.

She persisted, "Kerry, get Dr. Sideris in here now to assess for surgery."

Kerry was the hospitalist on rotation that day. I had met most of the doctors on the floor because of all our past visits, but I had never met her. She was a petite, quiet woman, and she was carefully and thoughtfully digesting all this information. This debate about Tim's immediate next step was heated, fueled by ego. I observed that Dr. Anderson felt threatened and upset that a nurse was trying to usurp his authority and therefore was holding on more tightly to his initial decision, even though it seemed obvious to everyone that he was wrong.

The conversation in the hospital room became heated, fueled by egos. The exception was Nurse Mary, the voice of reason. She pleaded that, ethically, she could not administer more morphine. Her arguments were authentic and rose above the cacophony. I was pacing, sobbing, and begging for everyone to listen to Mary. And I was terrified that she would be overruled and that I had no say in the situation of my very own son! I felt completely powerless.

The more I witnessed, the more overwrought I became, until Dr. Anderson finally turned to me. I thought he was going to acknowledge my authority as the patient's mother, but instead he said, "Get her out of the room. She's not helping things."

Even in a frantic state, I knew the moments were precious. Instead of arguing with Dr. Anderson, I wanted to use this time and my efforts more wisely.

Out of the room, I called Jill. Jill was our primary nurse when Tim was in NICU, and she and I remained close friends.

I never called my nurse friends because I didn't want them to think I was using them for medical advice because I was sincere in our friendship. But in this case, I couldn't afford to worry about this. Jill was truly my friend, and I needed help.

"Jill, Tim has a bowel obstruction. He has been sedated for twenty-four hours as they suctioned him. The doctors are debating about surgery. One of the nurses just said that if they keep giving him more morphine, he might code. Jill," I sobbed, "they are speaking a different language, and I don't know what to do and I am so tired. Please, help me." Jill didn't hesitate. She came to the hospital to be my "translator" and advocate. Now, years later, I wonder: Could Jill have lost her job by doing this? She was an employee at the hospital at the time, and I would think that this could jeopardize her career, yet she got in her car right away and was standing beside me within thirty minutes.

While I waited for Jill, I still was not allowed in the room while Chris worked with the medical team. My sister-in-law, Jennifer, had come to the hospital, and she was tasked with walking me around the block to calm me down.

This was my Road to Emmaus moment. In the story, two travelers walked away from Jerusalem, defeated from the death of Jesus, baffled by his disappearance from the tomb, and disheartened that Jesus did not save Israel. They were walking away from it all because all hope was lost. I too walked away—from the hospital room, from Tim, and from my hope. Along the way, the travelers meet someone who walks and talks with them until they got to the village of Emmaus. And only then did they realize it was Jesus walking with them the entire time. Like the travelers, I didn't realize as I walked away, God was walking with me in this dark moment and that, while the situation seemed hopeless and chaotic, there was hope.

Meanwhile, my mother-in-law, Susan, called my parents in Boston. They were at a Bruins game, picked up the phone, and were stunned to hear that Tim was so critically ill. My mom called me immediately while Jennifer and I were walking. "Katie, Susan just called. She was hysterical. I thought you said Tim had a bowel obstruction but that it was under control. Is she being dramatic? What is going on here?"

"No, Mom. She's not overblowing this. Tim is really, really sick. He has a very serious bowel obstruction, and one nurse thinks that if we keep giving him morphine, he may code," I whimpered. "Mom, I'm so scared. Mom, what if he doesn't live? Mom, I can't do this. I can't do this."

I could hear her weep softly. She just couldn't believe it. She put my dad on the phone. "Katie, is Tim that sick? What is going on?"

I explained the situation. "Dad, I can't lose him. I can't lose him. I can't lose him." At this point, I was thinking of how we went from complete normalcy a week ago to now where I could possibly be purchasing a tiny coffin. *Surreal* is not the right adjective to describe the situation: *hellish* was more like it.

My dad spoke some of the wisest, most compassionate words I have ever heard in my life. "Katie, I am just so sorry. I don't know the right words to say. I know that you have always struggled to get attached to Tim because you were afraid he wouldn't live. You never said it, but I've always known it. And now, you—and all of us—are completely attached to him. We know and love him. He is a part of us. I don't know why God does this. It's why life is such a mystery. It's beyond human comprehension. I am so sorry."

My dad's real talk, with no BS nor platitudes, revealed a truth buried deeply within the core of my soul that I didn't want to expose: I was always terrified to get too close to Tim in case he didn't live. It was the reason behind my workaholic tendencies during my pregnancy; the force behind my cheerful facade in NICU. The sheer exhaustion of our new-normal life never allowed me time to think about how traumatized and messed up I was from all that had happened. Throughout it all, I had been scared to attach to Tim.

There it was, out in the open. This new knowledge didn't give me peace in that moment, but it did give me a sense of perspective: as humans we can try as hard as we want, but we can't and don't control anything. Suffering inevitably happens to everyone and it will never, ever make sense to us. None of this—and I mean *none*—could possibly make sense.

I wish it wasn't this way and I wish I could tie it all up in a beautiful bow and explain it, but I can't. And no one can, no matter how smart or wise one thinks one is.

I can't say my dad's talk gave me strength either. But it snapped me out of hysteria and into a haze of sad acceptance. I was powerless. I needed God. I needed Him really badly. So I prayed to Him for the second time that day—the second time in months—to save my precious baby boy. It was all I could do. *God, please come back to me. Please save my baby boy. Please, I beg your intercession to save my little baby boy.* Like before with the miracle of the little girl, I was Jairus, running to Jesus, to heal my child once again.

Meanwhile, the verdict was decided: immediate, urgent surgery.

Relief flooded my body and hope flowed back into my body, soul, and heart. Thank God that Dr. Anderson was overruled. In my gut, I knew there was no way Tim could tolerate even a few more hours of suction and morphine. After all, this wasn't just a few hours of obstruction, this had been going on for a week—after two misdiagnoses.

Dr. Sideris, a key surgeon on Dr. Shapiro's team who had worked with Dr. Shapiro on all of Tim's previous surgeries, anxiously waited for us to sign all the paperwork to get into surgery. She briefly explained her strategy for surgery as well as potential risk: necrotic intestine.

"My goal is to remove the blockage. And my biggest hope is that none of his intestine became necrotic, or dusky, which would mean I have to remove part of it," she quickly explained to us.

"What does *necrotic* mean?" I asked.

Dr. Sideris quickly responded, "It's like if you keep a tight rubber band on your wrist too long and cut off your circulation. For Tim, we hope that the blockage isn't like that tight rubber band. We hope we caught this soon enough that blood continued to flow so that I don't have to remove part of the intestine. But I will only know when I go in."

I didn't Google anything, nor did I ask Jill what consequences a necrotic intestine may yield; I just knew that I trusted Dr. Sideris with my heart and soul. I did not allow myself to relive the past two incorrect diagnoses of a "stomach bug," nor did I get too far ahead on what would happen if part of Tim's intestines were removed. We had a solution, and I knew it was the proper course of action. Chris and I knew that the benefits far, far exceeded the risk. We gave her the green light.

My flicker of faith reignited. I felt God working through Dr. Sideris in these moments—through her confidence, honesty, brilliance, and skill as a surgeon. "Please, God, grant her wisdom in her decisions and dexterity in her hands as she fixes my precious baby boy, Timothy," I prayed over and over again. I can see now that God's persistent protection and intervention (the holy roar, the swift and unprecedented hospital exchange, my own walk to Emmaus) was unnoticed by me, but He was so, so close to me all this time, even when I thought to "unfriend" Him during Tim's infection, which seemed ages ago now.

The surgery, at four hours, was by far the longest surgery Chris, Tim, and I endured. Then Dr. Sideris came out of the OR around eleven thirty p.m. with a big smile. "Tim is a rock star. He tolerated surgery beautifully. And I didn't have to remove any part of the intestine." It was the best outcome we could have hoped for. She continued, "I took out his entire intestine, feet after feet of it, and gently unkinked it. That's what happens during a blockage; a part of the intestine gets kinked up like a garden hose kinks and cuts off the water supply. But we caught it soon enough, and he will be just fine."

I wept tears of joy. Pure joy.

Then I, at nearly six feet tall, nearly tackled petite Dr. Sideris with my embrace. "Thank you, Dr. Sideris. I can't thank you enough. I am so grateful for your brilliance and your steady hands. Thank you."

Dr. Sideris simply replied, "You're welcome. Now, he will recover. And you will see that babies bounce back very quickly." And we were brought to the Pediatric Intensive Care Unit (PICU) for recovery.

Bringing Tim to recover in the PICU was not the normal routine for such a situation. But while Tim was in surgery,

I begged to be transferred to PICU and not the pediatric floor. "We need more attention. Tim needs more acute care. We need nurses who can monitor him twenty-four seven. That doesn't happen on the pediatric floor because there are too many patients. Please, we must be transferred to PICU."

I often wonder if the hospital administrators thought my request was a little crazy. Not many parents ask for their child to be in intensive care. But I knew too much. Tim needed the acute care even in recovery. Or maybe, I was the one who needed the critical care. I also knew that if Tim were in PICU, Chris and I could sleep easier at night because it's quieter and calmer on the ICU floors.

We were granted the request, and Tim recovered in PICU for the next four days. He was intubated for twenty-four hours after the surgery, then he had the breathing tube removed, and gradually he became his active, happy self. Within four days, Tim went from a lethargic baby near death to a boisterous nine-month-old, nearly crawling out of his hospital bed. It was a modern-day miracle.

It took me years to realize how God was with us the whole time during the bowel obstruction. And it took me a long time because I blocked it out. Tim nearly died. For years, I would not allow myself to relive the scariest part of our story. And it was God's persistent protection of which I was unaware: the extraordinary action to get Tim back to WRPH after two misdiagnoses, our need for rest at exactly the right time, the shift change with Miracle Mary, Jill's presence and intervention, and prayers and support of our inner circle of family and friends, near and far.

When I reflect on Tim's extraordinary beginning, I can't help but be astounded by the countless miracles we experienced. Never did I think, in September 2014 at that eventful twenty-week ultrasound, that we would experience all that we did.

Tim proved to be a strong baby and tolerated major surgeries in NICU beyond the prebirth predictions. We left NICU months earlier than expected. While I thought that NICU was the finish line, it proved to be only the commencement of the life of a medically fragile baby. It didn't seem like it at the time, but I see how lucky we were that the on-call nurse heard Tim's oversized cough at just four months old and told us to quickly come into the hospital. And while the RSV lingered and an infection invaded Tim's Gore-Tex patch, we may not have spotted that right away if we hadn't already been in the hospital.

The exceptional whiplash of a critically ill baby battling a bowel obstruction to a bubbly, active baby amazed me. Tim recovered beautifully from surgery. He was discharged at four days and participated in his first Halloween, dressed up as a pediatric surgeon, naturally. Most friends outside our inner circle, didn't even know that all of this had happened because I didn't have the words to describe it to them.

It's difficult to express what kind of miracles we experienced, so almost no one really knew about it. Until now. Now, it seems impossible *not* to see the divine hand and timing of it all.

Years later, a colleague said to me, "Always trust in divine timing."

And after all I've been through, I emphatically reply, "I do!"

I think one of the biggest challenges and mysteries I had, in all my suffering, was to receive the mercy and grace of God. I recounted several reflections on what suffering means and how we can't understand the will of God, no matter how hard we try. And nothing sums it up better than a conversation I had in the chaos of the debate among the medical team during Tim's bowel obstruction. I had called Molleen, my childhood best friend and rock during NICU, and sobbed, "Molleen, we have been through so much, and Tim has survived and always bounced back. But this bowel obstruction is scaring me. We have gotten so many miracles. But this . . . is this the time that our miracles run out?"

Maybe I thought miracles were earned through faith. Or that miracles were given to the worthy. Or that there were only so many miracles God could perform in a year. Or that I hadn't been grateful enough for the many miracles already granted to us, to Tim.

But Molleen responded, "Katie, God doesn't work like that. Miracles don't run out. There are infinite miracles."

EPILOGUE

2023

"Oh, my gosh, Jill. I can't believe you called. It's been for-ever. Hey, I just got home from a wicked-late lacrosse game. Can I call you tomorrow?"

"Yes, call me after nine p.m. your time."

I called Nurse Jill the following night.

"Hey, Jill, did you see the Instagram post? *Infinite Miracles* will be published soon."

"That's great!" she replied.

"Wait, isn't that why you called?" Many friends from that period of my life had been texting and calling because of the announcement.

"No. I'm not on Instagram—I didn't see anything. At work people were talking about omphaloceles, and I thought of you, so that's why I called."

Jill and I hadn't talked since 2019—other than through Christmas cards. But today, out of the blue, she called me. Yet another little coincidence, a sweet nudge from the Holy Spirit. Jill was one of the very first to be with me on my NICU journey, and now, as I was wrapping up a memoir about it all, here she was.

"How are the boys? How is Tim?" Jill asked.

"Well . . ."

My second son, PJ, was born in 2018. Chris and I sadly divorced in 2019, and we decided it was best that I move back East to Massachusetts, close to my family, with the boys. Of course, in these circumstances, I couldn't be a stay-at-home mom and, fortunately, landed back into my career, thanks to Sharon (Remember the office baby shower? That Sharon!) in a role that fits me better than before.

Over time, Tim, PJ, and I settled into a little family of three, with the help of my parents, and adjusted to life in New England. They started day care and school, sports; and we all made our own little circle of friends and developed a rock-solid routine. As the boys settled into life in Massachusetts, they, especially PJ, developed a hint of a Boston accent with certain words.

Tim is now eight years old, thriving at his Catholic school, and he loves to read more than anything else, mostly the original *Hardy Boys* books. He is also quite an athlete. He plays soccer, hockey, and lacrosse. He loves whatever sport is in season, but I think he has a gift for hockey. And it goes back to the toughness that he's had since NICU. I remember calling Dr. Shapiro all the way from Massachusetts, asking him if Tim could safely play such a physical sport. He simply replied, "Yes. He's tough." So I signed him up for Learn to Skate, and it's been rink life since then. It's hard to believe that my fragile baby is now banging the boards in competitive Massachusetts youth hockey.

PJ, my second son who is now five, is a sweet, funny little boy who loves puzzles, Legos, and putting stuff together.

Tim isn't the only one who is tough, as PJ often reminds me. "I don't need a jacket for school or T-ball," he explains when the weather might suggest otherwise. PJ and Tim are best friends: giggling about their secret sports cave; beating each other up, as only brothers can do; playing mini sticks (hockey with small sticks) in the basement; and promising not to tattle on one another.

And then there's me. After a triple whammy of NICU, divorce, and the isolation of life during COVID, I'm okay now. And I've come out of it all with gratitude. I realize it may seem crazy that I have gratitude after all this hardship, but I do. I never want to relive those tough times, nor do I wish them upon anyone, but the lessons from my hardships are more valuable than any huge house or luxury car. In fact, my ordeals have left me with far less, materially, than many of my peers, but I often wonder if I have more gratitude for the small things as well as a more unique perspective than others because of all that I went through.

One way I healed was quitting social media—cold turkey! I was off all social media from 2020 until 2023. During NICU, it was hard to stay disciplined with social media intake, but during COVID, it felt darn near impossible because there was so little life outside the home. We "lived" on our smartphones (which isn't living). I found myself comparing myself to others, envious of their seemingly perfect lives, while I was struggling just to get to baseline. So, I took the social media apps off all my devices and went social media–free for many years. I wonder if being free of the addictive comparison feedback loop accelerated my healing.

I attended therapy. Therapy helped me, and I was blessed to have a good therapist. But remote therapy due to COVID just wasn't cutting it. I found that I dreaded those telephone sessions, not through any fault of my therapist, but teletherapy, instead of in-person, reminded me of my profound isolation and lack of intimacy due to divorce and life during COVID.

I had to find God. Or maybe, God had to find me. In January 2021, Tony Dungy and Ben Watson of the Indianapolis Colts wrote an opinion piece in the *Wall Street*

Journal about being faithful in a pandemic and calling to action for a Christian revival. I thought to myself, *I want to be a part of this! I'm faithful, right? But do I even know what being faithful is anymore?*

I embarked on Bible Study. By myself. I bought a study guide on Amazon, cracked open the Bible, and started with the first book, Genesis. I approached this endeavor not expecting to get spiritual enlightenment; I just needed the background knowledge of the biblical stories in order to figure out how to be a good Christian and be faithful. And as if I was a second grader tackling a reading comprehension assignment, I read Scripture and neatly answered the questions in my study guide.

Then, that's where the magic began. The stories flowed, and I needed to keep going. *What happens next*, I asked myself as I moved onto Exodus and then, Leviticus, Numbers, and Deuteronomy. My Old Testament study guides referenced Scripture from the New Testament, and I started to see connections between the two. I couldn't help but skip around and go to the Gospels and the Letters, and then go back to the Old Testament stories. I would find a commentator who suggested other references and read those too or watch YouTube videos that explained the stories and meaning. I devoured all this knowledge. And of course, I had time to do this because I was liberated from the social media time-suck.

I'm not sure that I had deep religious perspective when I was going through everything. But many years later, I can see and feel that God was with me during that infamous sonogram, during the pregnancy, when Tim was born, in that NICU room, back with us for every subsequent hospital issue, there for us when Tim recovered and healed. During my divorce, God had more storms for me that required a different healing process with more privacy and different coping methods, but He was there. And He was there for me as we all endured the collective isolation (not an oxymoron) of COVID. I was utterly broken for a long time and didn't know where to turn until I found Him through my simple, self-made, "second grade" Bible Study.

God fixed me, this broken woman, and made me whole by His grace.

Jill and I shifted the conversation back to her. We talked about her new job and life, closer to her own family, in the Midwest. Our conversation went well past my usual bedtime in the Eastern time zone.

As we wrapped up our call, even though we had more to talk about, I told Jill, "I still can't believe you called—now of all times."

"I know—crazy how life is, right?"

And it is. Ten years ago, the most devastating news struck me like a thunderbolt on that sonogram table. I couldn't imagine how I would ever endure such a situation. But little did I know the countless angels in my life and how infinitely interconnected our lives were and are. I—and all the friends, family, and medical team—could never have imagined such a regular life back in 2015. More like, we would never have let ourselves imagine this day. But here it was—miraculous in its simplicity.

REFLECTION ON NICU FEELINGS GUIDE

For NICU Parents: If you don't have time to read the entire book but would like to read about common issues and themes in NICU, here is a simple guide to the places each theme is explored at greater length in the memoir.

Expectations

∞ Shattering expectations about the baby you thought you would have instead of who your baby is (pages 11–13)

∞ The grief of snuggle-free parenthood in NICU (pages 85–90 and 94–95)

∞ Marriage through good times and bad (pages 126–130)

∞ Expectations are premeditated resentments (page 162)

Coping with being broken-hearted (anger, sadness, and suffering)

∞ Letting go of entitlement (pages 14–16)

∞ Begging for reasons for the suffering (pages 14–16)

Coping with being broken-hearted (anger, sadness, and suffering), cont.

Dealing with friends and family

Prayer

∞ Prayer as light in the darkness (pages 17–18)

∞ Prayer plan through friendship (pages 33–35)

∞ The power of communal prayer (pages 37–39)

∞ Bible study (pages 223–225)

Depression/anxiety/fear

∞ Keeping busy (page 36)

∞ Worrying about money (pages 59–60)

∞ Feeling numb (page 92)

∞ Helplessness by choice (page 145)

∞ When everything is out of control
   (pages 164–168)

MORE EXPERIENCES

The following are references to more personal stories that you may find comfort in. If you're struggling with any of the topics below, choose a story and flip to that chapter.

Motherhood

∞ My longing to become a mom (pages 24–25)

Motherhood, cont.

∞ Mother Mary's difficult entry to motherhood (pages 67–68)

∞ Being a mom: Not about me! (pages 79–80)

∞ Bonding with baby: The grief of snuggle-free parenthood in NICU (pages 85–90 and 94–95)

∞ Mary #2: Breastfeeding (pages 105–107)

∞ I'm not worthy (pages 155–157)

Surrender/trust

∞ Meeting my medical dream team (pages 43–49)

∞ Taking off my necklaces (pages 75–77)

∞ Mary #1: Nana in the room with me (pages 78–79)

∞ Relax, everything is out of control (pages 164–168)

∞ Unfriending God (but He didn't unfriend me) (pages 175–176)

∞ My own road to Emmaus (pages 210–211)

Acceptance

∞ Not the path I wanted, but the path I got (pages 23–25)

∞ There is no finish line in life (page 149)

∞ Must accept (pages 170–171)

Joy/humor

∞ The cry of life (page 79)

∞ Humor as the antidote to anxiety (pages 80–81)

∞ The healing miracle: Skin closure (pages 101–103)

∞ Mary #2: Breastfeeding (pages 105–107)

∞ Choose the better part (page 146)

∞ What is a miracle? (pages 218–219)

Compassion of strangers

∞ The nurse was the light of my world (pages 87–89)

∞ You are my neighbor (pages 96–97)

∞ The other Katie from Massachusetts
(pages 131–132)

∞ Mary #2: Breastfeeding (pages 105–107)

∞ Stop! We need an ultrasound! (page 180)

∞ Flight for Life: Not all heroes wear capes,
sometimes they wear blue jumpsuits
(page 200–201)

∞ God's persistent protection and intervention
(pages 216–217)

∞ Mary #3: Miracle Mary (pages 204–208)

Anxiety into peace, calm, and comfort

∞ Matthew 5:4

∞ Matthew 6:34

∞ Matthew 8:26

∞ Matthew 11:28

Sadness, weakness into strength

∞ Luke 1:79

∞ 2 Corinthians 12:9–10

∞ Philippians 4:14

∞ 2 Timothy 1:7

Lament: expressing anger, bitterness

∞ Job 7:11

∞ Job 10:1–2

∞ Job 16:8

∞ Psalm 22:1–2

Rocky roads to motherhood

∞ Genesis 21:2

∞ Matthew 2:13–18

∞ Luke 1:18

∞ Luke 1:26–38

∞ Luke: 2: 1–12

Power of prayer

∞ Psalm 27:14

∞ Psalm 116:6

∞ Psalm 141:1–2

∞ Psalm 141:1–2

∞ Matthew 6: 9–13

Joy

∞ Job 37:5

∞ Psalm 118:24

∞ Proverbs 27:9

Joy, cont.

∞ Ecclesiastes 3:14; 4

∞ Zephaniah 3:17

Healing

∞ Ezekiel 36:26

∞ Mark 5:23–24, 36–42

Love, compassion, and friendship

∞ Lamentations 3:32

∞ Matthew 5:14–16

∞ Matthew 5:44

∞ Luke 10:27

∞ Luke 10: 41–42

∞ John 15:13

Hope

∞ Luke 24:13–35

∞ Romans 5:3–5

Thanksgiving and praise to God

∞ Psalm 100:1

∞ Psalm 111:1–2

Trust in God, He knows us and never leaves our sides

∞ Exodus 29:46

∞ Leviticus 23:42–43

∞ Psalm 23:4

∞ Psalm 37:3–5

∞ Psalm 42:1

∞ Proverbs 20:18

∞ Isaiah 43:1

∞ Isaiah 55:8–9

∞ Jeremiah 10:23

∞ Matthew 4:19

∞ Mark 14:36

∞ Luke 15:3–7

Trust in God, He knows us and never leaves our side, cont.

∞ John 15:16

∞ John 1:14

∞ John 14:2–7

∞ John 15:9

∞ John 14:6

ACKNOWLEDGMENTS

I would like to express my gratitude for all the people in my life who made this book happen. *Infinite Miracles* would not be written if not for very special people in my life who encouraged, supported, listened (and put up with me) during the NICU journey and writing process.

I'll go backward and start with the people who most recently encouraged and supported me. I'll begin with those partnered with me in the writing process.

I would like to thank my developmental editor, Skye Levy, who I met through one of my best friends and roommate from Holy Cross, Kaitlin Herlihy, over ten years ago in Boulder, CO. Over the years, Skye and I had many mutual friends and we always saw each other at dinners, parties, and crazy road races that only happen in Boulder! After Tim was born, I posted on Facebook that I was journaling–and possibly writing a memoir—about Tim. I wanted to write his birth story down before I forgot things. Skye read one of these posts and DM'd me, "Katie, you have something here." And from there, and over the course of three years (with much time off in between our work), Skye was there gently pushing me to dig deeper, connecting the different parts of the story, organizing my ideas, and encouraging me the entire time. Skye is a gifted writer, storyteller, and mentor. It is not hyperbole to say *Infinite Miracles* would not be written if not for my partnership with Skye. Skye was not only my developmental editor but my biggest cheerleader and friend. Skye, thank you for everything. And thank you, Kaitlin, for introducing us!

There is a group of special women who picked up for me when my time with Skye was complete. I had no idea what to do after the manuscript was complete. I didn't know about all the moving parts of self-publishing a book!

But one thing I did know is that one of the most important parts of a self-published book is a beautiful book cover. The book cover must evoke the feeling of the book, flow together seamlessly, and captivate a reader from afar. Tall order, right? Enter Emily Hoyt. I found Emily's artwork on Instagram and was inspired by her faith and talent. I messaged her to see if she designed and created book covers and she said yes. We scheduled a phone call; she intently listened to my story and my vision for the book and created a book cover more beautiful than I could have envisioned. Thank you, Emily, for your vision and talent.

I met Ines Monnet, my book formatter, also through social media. I didn't know much, but I knew that book formatting—how the book is laid out—is an art. And while I have many skills, I knew I would never figure out how to format a book. And if by some miracle I did figure it out, it would look like a mess! Ines had all the answers, expertise, and assurance that we could do this together. And she also had a lot of referrals for the final steps of the book publishing process. Thank you, Ines, for making my book so beautiful and connecting me to so many talented people.

Ines introduced me to Carly Catt, my copy editor. Oh yes! There's another type of editor after Skye, the developmental editor. The copy editor makes sure the book is grammatically correct and flows coherently. I asked Carly to do a sample edit, and she turned it around in less than a day. It was spectacular. I wondered if she somehow channeled my former grammar teacher from seventh grade due to her precision and knowledge of her revisions. We partnered right away. Carly carefully combed over the manuscript to makes sure everything in *Infinite Miracles* is grammatically correct and flows well. I knew my book would be polished, professional, and perfect. Carly, thank you.

Susi Clark was the next person Ines recommended for making decisions and managing all the moving parts of distribution. Susi and I met on Zoom, and again, it was an instant partnership. She gave me valuable information about the pros and cons of different options and helped me understand all the pre-publication duties and how to do the final and important last-minute details of a book launch. Thank you, Susi, for bringing me to the finish line.

I didn't realize it as I was writing – and I am grateful for this temporary state of blissful ignorance – that the marketing part of self-publishing can be just as long or longer than writing the actual book! Skye put me in touch with Claudine Wolk. Fitting with my theme of divine timing, Claudine's book, *Get Your Book Seen and Sold* came out right when I was deciding the timeline of my book launch. And thank God for that book. I learned that I would change my book launch date to have proper time for a less frantic and more fun marketing roll-out.

This extended timeline gave me time to do a few important marketing tasks—that turned out to be a blast. I made an appointment for head shots, so I had professional pictures of myself, the new author (it still feels weird to say it!). I called Elise Travis, our family photographer, and she couldn't wait for the assignment. I scheduled a hair appointment with fabulous Robin LeBoeuf and makeup with Nena. Elise snapped away in her studio for an hour. I felt transformed that day and so grateful for Elise, Robin, and Nene who made me feel so beautiful and special. Thank you, Elise, Robin, and Nena.

Another exciting part of the marketing plan was designing my own author website. I partnered with Jenny Medford at Websy Daisy to create a digital home. I worked with Jenny years before on a website for another project. She is professional and talented. The new author website she designed for me is exactly what I envisioned. Thank you, Jenny.

While all this work was happening, I had many friends encouraging and supporting me. I'd like to thank Ashling Besgen. Ashling and I reconnected at our twentieth Holy Cross reunion, and she became one of my best friends. Ashling patiently listened to me describe the challenges of writing while being a full-time working mom. She has supported and pushed me at those moments when I just wanted to say, "Why bother with this whole thing?" Thank you, Ash, for always being there.

There are two other Holy Cross Crusaders I'd like to thank: Lisa B. and Rob Poulin. Lisa was my constant support throughout NICU. She is my colleague, friend, faith mentor, and the big sister I never had. She introduced me to Rob so I could learn about self-publishing. Rob took time out of his hectic work–and Patriots fan–schedule to spend hours on the phone with me guiding me with all the steps of self-publishing. Thank you, Rob, for your invaluable knowledge, advice, and guidance.

I'd like to thank all my friends from my two main communities: school and hockey. The moms at my boys' school and the hockey moms have been my biggest cheerleaders. I am so grateful for their interest in my work and support for me. I want to especially thank Kristen Murawski, Karla and Todd Hanna for not only always being there for me but helping with specific tasks to roll out the book.

Before school and hockey, there was my NICU community. I don't know if I could have gotten through NICU without Amanda, Lindsay F., Liz, and Molleen. Words can hardly capture how grateful I am for your friendship and kindness through one of the hardest storms of my life. I also want to thank others who were there in the aftermath of NICU: Renee, Lindsay K., Ashleigh S., Deb, Judy, Ashley T., Sarah, Lucia, Mary Ellen, Christina, Britt, Jess, Lindsay A., Libby, Victoria, and Denae. You were my support during those critical months of healing when things finally stabilized physically but the emotional challenges just started. Thank you for being there.

My time in NICU and that challenging first year after Tim was born was made a little easier by the empathy and compassion of my work family at Houghton Mifflin Harcourt. Thank you, Mike, Kyle, John, and Tim for giving me flexibility during a very challenging time. And thank you to my dear friends and colleagues in the NY office and Rocky Mountain offices, Angela Gitto and Jennifer Baley, who always checked in on me before, during, and after NICU. I also want to thank my current work family at Savvas Learning for being supportive of me while I wrote the book (well after work hours!). Thank you to the New England sales team: Steve, John, Mia, Sharon, Shaun, Tippy, Sandra, Greer, Ashley, Jackie, Melanie, Sarah, and Jason. You are the best!

I'd like to thank the high-risk nurses who cared for me, especially Barbara. I'd also like to thank the NICU of our children's hospital, especially the pediatric surgery team and the neonatologists. You healed my critically sick baby. I am forever in gratitude of your brilliant minds and healing hands. I especially want to thank our primary nurse, Jill, who is a lifelong friend. She was there for us at the very beginning and helped us with every major milestone of Tim's eventful babyhood.

I'd like to thank my ex-husband, Chris, for being my partner during NICU. Though our lives took a turn apart from one another, I feel grateful we found each other and had our beautiful boys together. Thank you, Chris, for your support—and recollections—in the writing of Tim's extraordinary birth story.

I like to thank my mom's "gang" in Massachusetts: Betsy, Lisa, Rita, Jane, Marie, Kim, and Carol. Betsy calmed and reassured me when we received the omphalocele diagnosis. I am forever grateful for you, Betsy, for being so steady and composed in one of my darkest moments. Lisa, Rita, Jane,

Marie, Kim, and Carol—thank you for being there for my mom as she was going through NICU as a grandmother. Thank you to all of you for being the role model of what it is a to be a strong mother: able to endure hardship, love life, raise confident, adventurous children, and always keep a sense of humor and style all the while.

I'd like to thank my family for their endless support, love, kindness, laughs, and strong faith. Lizzie, thank you for being the best sister and Auntie Lizard to the boys. You always know how to give hugs at the right time and how to make me laugh in even the most unbelievable moments. Andrew, Sara, Charlotte, Gigi, and Margot, thank you for being the best brother/sister-in-law/nieces I could ever have. Your love for life is infectious, and I only wish we lived closer to each other. As a boy mom, there's not a lot of glitter in the day-to-day; you girls (including Andrew) add glitter and sparkle to my life.

Auntie Kathy, Uncle Larry, Morgan, Joe, and Alex—thank you for your encouragement, support, and inspiration. Alex, boy am I glad you selected a college out west so I had family in the area—and frequent visits from your mom and dad—while I was going through everything. Auntie Susan and Uncle Kevin, thank you for checking in about the book and encouraging me for my progress. Thank you to the O'Hagan family for being my "family by friendship". You always support and encourage me.

Mom and Dad, I feel blessed to have you as my parents, and I hope to be as strong a role model for my children as you are to me. Your love of life, huge community of friends, and unshakable faith are truly an inspiration to me.

And last—thank you to my sons, Tim and PJ. I feel blessed and grateful that God chose me to be your mom. You are the lights of my life. I cherish each moment with you both and can't wait for many, many (and hopefully, less dramatic) adventures together! I love you both so much.

ABOUT THE AUTHOR

Katie Simons McCarty grew up in Massachusetts. She attended the College of the Holy Cross and earned her master's degree from Mercy College through the New York City Teaching Fellows. She lived in Boston and New York City for fifteen years, working as an educator and in educational publishing. Katie moved to Denver for a change of pace and energy.

Katie comes from a family with the gift of the gab, full of comedians and storytellers. Inspired by her family and their creative endeavors, she started a humorous health and fitness blog in 2011. When her first son, Tim was born in 2015 with a rare birth defect called an omphalocele, she spent two months in NICU. After this life-changing event, Katie shifted her writing and focus to helping other NICU families.

Katie has been a guest-blogger on several mom blogs and she was a guest on the podcast, *Mighty Littles*, which focuses on parenting in the NICU. Katie also worked for Toby's Shower for Babies, which donates gift baskets for NICU families. She was the keynote speaker for their 2016 gala.

The birth of PJ in 2018 completed their little family. Life brought Katie and her two boys to back to Massachusetts in 2019 and they are happy to be near family. They love superheroes, hockey, and cheering for the Boston Bruins.

Infinite Miracles is Katie's debut book.

- ∞ **Subscribe to Katie Simons McCarty's email list at** www.katiesimonsmccarty.com.

- ∞ **To discuss booking Katie Simons McCarty for media or speaking events, email** katie.simons77@gmail.com

- ∞ **Website:** www.katiesimonsmccarty.com

- ∞ **Facebook:** @katiesimonsmccarty

- ∞ **Instagram:** @katie_simons_mccarty

Printed in the USA
CPSIA information can be obtained
at www.ICGtesting.com
JSHW021057120524
62888JS00004B/23

9 798989 506606